The Nature of Law for AQA and I

Concepts of law and legal theories illustrat
substantive law and legal

Sally Russell LLB (Hons), PG

- Key features
- Tasks and self-test questions throughout (answers at www.drsr.org)
- Evaluation pointers
- Examples to bring the law to life
- Clear explanations of the various concepts of law with modern examples
- Connections to the substantive law
- Summaries and diagrams for the main points of each area
- Examinations tips and question practice

My main objective has been to combine legal accuracy with a style that is accessible to all students, so I hope you will find this book both stimulating and helpful. Fully updated with recent cases and laws it is written in a lively, clear and accessible way and is designed to help students of all learning styles to understand the subject. The book is written for AQA and Eduqas but covers the A level specifications for most examination boards. AQA would only give approval to one publisher so this book does not carry an official badge of approval from them. However the AQA Portfolio Curriculum team kindly gave help and advice on content and assessment and I am grateful to them.

Although aimed at A Level the book provides a good base for 1st Year LLB, CILEx and other courses, and can be used as a self-study guide.

Other books by Sally Russell

As new books may be available by the time you read this I have not listed my other books by title. They currently include crime and tort at AS and A2 level for both the AQA and OCR examination boards. Also *'the law explained'* series offers a more in-depth coverage of individual areas with additional tasks, examples and examination practice. These cover much of crime and tort as well as various concepts of law. This means you can pick those topics for which you need more guidance (all the answers to tasks are included in the booklets).

For the most up-to-date list of what is available please check my author's page on Amazon or visit my website at www.drsr.org. All my books are available in both Kindle and paperback.

There is a list of some common abbreviations in the appendix at the end of the book.

Acknowledgements

With thanks to the AQA Portfolio Curriculum Team for their help and support in interpretation of the 2017 specifications and to my husband Dave for the diagrams and proof-reading.

Table of contents

Introduction

The nature of law is *synoptic*. This means it connects to the other areas you study, not just the substantive law, but the institutions and procedures too. When considering the nature of law and legal concepts you need to look at the rest of your course from a different perspective. You will be expected to show your understanding of the nature of law by relating the other topics you study to the more theoretical concepts found here.

For AQA, the focus is on the link between the nature of law and the substantive law (crime, tort, contract and human rights) in all three papers. For Eduqas the focus is on the link between the nature of law and the non-substantive law (law making and the English legal system) in Component 1. Each chapter includes examples from both the substantive and non-substantive law which should be useful for all students. Eduqas students will find the substantive law examples helpful when evaluating the law for Component 3. AQA students will find the non-substantive law useful for evaluating law making and the legal system.

The theory of law is called *jurisprudence*, and is a compulsory part of most law degrees. The academics and judges who have written about these concepts will have tackled several of them so will appear in more than one chapter. There is much disagreement between them and you are not expected to 'take sides'. The main thing when it comes to the examination is to have a clear focus and keep your answer centred on the specific question asked, i.e., keep your answer and examples relevant and, where possible, use one or two of the theorists to support what you say.

The first chapter includes legal theory and the rule of law and introduces you to the nature of law with an overview of the various concepts. Much is repeated here from my A level books on the criminal law and tort because these general principles and the rule of law permeate all areas of law. It is important that you understand these but if you have used my books you can just use the first chapter as revision.

After this introduction each chapter will explain a concept in detail and provide examples connecting the nature of law to other areas of substantive law (crime etc.) and to legal procedures. The facts of the cases are not given in full where you should know these from studying the substantive law topic. The criminal law cases used to illustrate the concepts are based on my book Criminal Law for AQA AS and A Level but apply to other examination boards. Similarly the tort cases are based on Tort Law for AQA AS and A Level. These and the OCR books for crime and tort were all published in 2017. Human rights will be published in 2018.

The concepts covered in this book are:

Chapter 2: Law and morals

Chapter 3: Law and justice

Chapter 4: Law and society – the concept of fault

Chapter 5: Law and society – balancing competing interests

For AQA students these are allocated to the three papers as follows:

Law and society – fault: Papers 1 and 2

Law and society – balancing competing interests: Paper 3 (but note it is included in the substantive law for tort in relation to injunctions as a remedy)

Law and morality: Papers 2 and 3

Law and Justice: Papers 1 and 3

Although these concepts are assigned to a particular paper, you are not limited to using only that area of law to illustrate the concept. AQA have confirmed that you can use any areas of law to help to explain the concepts as long as you focus on any specific points raised by the question.

For Eduqas all four of the concepts come into component 1.

Chapter 1: The theory and nature of criminal and civil law and the rule of law

The word law in phrases such as the law of tort, criminal law, human rights law, contract law etc., refers to the substance of the law (hence these topics are called substantive law). The word law in a wider sense is a more elusive concept, as it relates to the nature rather than the substance of law (called non-substantive law). It involves consideration of what academics and judges think the nature of law is (and what it should be). This in itself involves consideration of theories of law, such as law and justice, law and morality, the role of law in society in relation to fault and balancing competing interests and the role of law in keeping up with and regulating new technology. When considering the nature of law you need to look at the rest of your course from a different perspective. Each chapter will explain the concept and provide examples from criminal and civil law to illustrate it.

Examination tip

Whichever examination board you are using you will generally be able to use examples and cases from across the specifications to illustrate these concepts. However, read the question carefully because you may be asked to refer to a particular law or procedure. If so make sure you relate your discussion of the theories to that law or procedure, but you can use any relevant cases to illustrate them. There are plenty to choose from in each chapter for all the concepts.

This first chapter will introduce you to the theory and nature of law and provide an overview of the various concepts. Following this is an example to show how the concepts apply in a given situation and how they overlap. The final part of the chapter is on the rule of law, an essential part of most law courses, though sometimes included with the English legal system rather than with the nature of law.

1.1 The role of law and legal liability

The law plays a role in society by regulating behaviour and establishing social control. It punishes those convicted of a crime and compensates the victims of any civil wrongdoing. It also facilitates (e.g., by giving powers to form contracts or get married) and protects (e.g., by laws against theft and violence, and data protection laws). Law can really only be understood in a wider social context. The law plays an important role in society not only in providing justice but also as a method of social control and of balancing competing interests (both public and private) to control the way society behaves. Law sometimes involves enforcing moral as well as legal rules. As a society becomes more developed and more diverse it has a wider range of moral standpoints. Another role of law involves developing the law to keep up with new technology, either through the courts or by passing an Act of Parliament. These are all concepts of law, or legal theories.

The nature of law is essentially that it is based on rules. However, this word is used in a wide sense and the law may encompass principles and policies as well as rules. Even in its simple sense the word rule is ambiguous when trying to define law. This is because legal rules share many characteristics with moral rules. We need to consider what distinguishes a legal rule from other rules (or norms) of behaviour and what makes a rule have the force of law. In order to attempt to differentiate between moral and legal rules various theories of law and justice have been suggested. There are two broad approaches. The positivist approach sees law and morals as separate. The natural law view sees law and morals as linked. The first looks at what law is and the second at what it ought to be. These are also theories of justice. This is what the next two chapters are about.

In order better to understand the nature of law we need to know a bit more about where the law comes from and how a person may become liable in law. Legal liability occurs when the rules have been broken, but there is a difference between civil and criminal liability.

Sources of Law

We are governed by rules imposed by the state and this involves the making of law. Law makers include judges who produce common law through cases heard in the higher courts, and Parliament which produces statute law. Some (not many) laws come from custom, i.e., they have been going on for so long they are accepted as law even though not set out in a case or statute. These are all sources of law. Other sources of law today include European law and Human Rights law.

All these areas are covered elsewhere in the course under law making and the English legal system.

Legal rules and legal liability

Social rules are often referred to as norms. A norm can be described as the expected standard of behaviour within a society. However both legal rules (law) and social rules (morals) are called norms by academics and lawyers. That is why it is important to be able to differentiate between law and morals (see Chapter 1). It is possible to say all rules are norms, but social norms are not enforced in law whereas legal norms are.

There is no agreed definition of law. Essentially, it is a matter of rules, but so is much a life. Therefore, a distinction needs to be made between enforceable legal rules and other norms of behaviour. There are many rules governing our lives but not all are enforceable. There may be rules governing how you behave in school or college, and there will be rules at home too. None of these rules has the force of law. A teacher or parent may punish (sanction) you for breaking these rules but there will be no such sanctions from a court of law.

Law is based on liability. A person is legally liable when accountable in law for something done or not done. There are two types of liability, criminal and civil, and both are based on the principle of individuals being responsible for their conduct.

Criminal liability is based on an individual's responsibility to the state and society as a whole.

Civil liability is based on an individual's responsibility to other individuals.

The main differences between criminal and civil liability are seen in the *consequences* not the deed. Harming someone is against the criminal law, but the victim (V) may want to sue in civil law to claim compensation for any injuries, thus there is both criminal and civil liability. Here is a summary of the different types of action in court:

Criminal Law

Proceedings are initiated by the Crown (Crown Prosecution Service)

Proceedings are paid for by the State

Cases commence in the Magistrates' Court

Serious crimes are heard in the Crown Court

The accused is prosecuted

The burden of proof is on the prosecution

The standard of proof is beyond reasonable doubt

The primary purpose is punishment

The case is in the form of R v Smith (R stands for Regina i.e., the Crown)

Civil Law

Proceedings are initiated by the individual (the claimant)

Proceedings are paid for by the parties (usually the loser)

Cases commence in the County Court or High Court depending on the amount claimed

The defendant is sued

The burden of proof is on the Claimant

The standard of proof is the balance of probabilities

The primary purpose is compensation, called damages

The case is in the form of Smith v Brown (i.e., the parties to the dispute)

If you prefer diagrams:

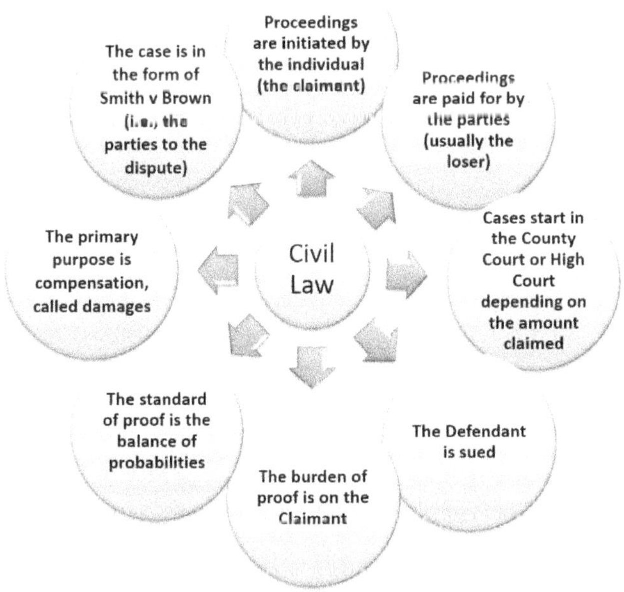
Proceedings are initiated by the individual (the claimant)
Proceedings are paid for by the parties (usually the loser)
Cases start in the County Court or High Court depending on the amount claimed
The Defendant is sued
The burden of proof is on the Claimant
The standard of proof is the balance of probabilities
The primary purpose is compensation, called damages
The case is in the form of Smith v Brown (i.e., the parties to the dispute)
Civil Law

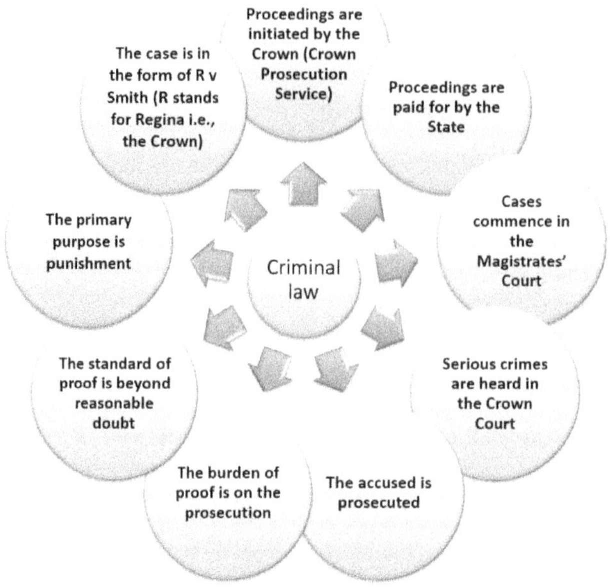
Proceedings are initiated by the Crown (Crown Prosecution Service)
Proceedings are paid for by the State
Cases commence in the Magistrates' Court
Serious crimes are heard in the Crown Court
The accused is prosecuted
The burden of proof is on the prosecution
The standard of proof is beyond reasonable doubt
The primary purpose is punishment
The case is in the form of R v Smith (R stands for Regina i.e., the Crown)
Criminal law

The nature of law differs between criminal law and civil liability so we will take a brief look at each separately.

The theory and nature of criminal law

There is no exact definition of a crime, but there are some fundamental principles which are accepted as being part of the nature of criminal law. The criminal law **prohibits** certain actions and **punishes** those who commit them.

The basic elements of criminal liability are **guilty conduct** (*actus reus*) and **guilty mind** (*mens rea*). These general elements of liability are basic principles of law. When making rules of criminal law certain other principles are upheld. One principle is that the law, especially criminal law, must be certain and the rules clearly defined. This is a requirement of both the rule of law and justice. It is often referred to as 'fair labelling' and there are several offences that are not sufficiently clearly defined, in particular the non-fatal offences against the person. The main basis for criminalising behaviour is harm. This is not only harm to a person but also harm to property, hence laws **prohibiting** violence and theft. The law expects people to be responsible for their actions, so **punishes** those who break the law if found to be at fault. This is the principle of individual autonomy. Individuals are deemed responsible for their own behaviour and this justifies imposing punishment on them for breaking the rules. There are different levels of fault in criminal law, but whatever the level of fault (*mens rea*), it is generally accepted that it should correspond with the conduct (*actus reus*). This means a person should only be criminally liable where the *mens rea* was for the offence actually committed. This principle is called the correspondence principle but it is not always followed in practice. Where there is no accordance, or correspondence, between the *actus reus* and *mens rea* it is known as constructive liability. There are examples of this with the substantive law you study as it applies to murder, manslaughter and two of the non-fatal offences against the person. Finally, it is generally accepted that the law should not be retrospective; it should apply to the future and not the past. This is the case with statute law passed by Parliament as that will prohibit behaviour from the time the Act becomes law. However, with the common law, which comes from judgments in cases, this is not always true because if the decision has changed the law, the person in court maybe guilty of something that was not previously illegal.

An example is the case of **R v R** discussed below.

The theory and nature of civil law

Civil liability occurs when someone has infringed the rights of another, e.g., has breached a contract. In tort there is a right not to be harmed and a right to enjoy one's property without interference. Both criminal and civil law are usually based on the principle of fault, so a person is not liable unless blameworthy. Both are also based on the principle of individual responsibility. However, as with the criminal law both these principles are just that, principles not rules. There are exceptions e.g., **Rylands v Fletcher 1868** is a tort which does not require fault and vicarious liability is where the employer is liable, not the individual who committed the tort.

The main purpose of the civil law is to compensate the claimant (C) by awarding a remedy against the defendant (D). This is usually in the form of monetary compensation (called damages) but may also be an injunction (to stop the wrongdoing).

Liability in tort is usually based on responsibility. However, sometimes it is based on policy. This means looking at the wider picture and at what is best for society as a whole. This is seen in particular with proving a duty of care in negligence. It also comes into the remedy of an injunction.

Tort is an important part of the civil law and protects a wide range of interests. These include physical harm (to a person or to property), psychiatric harm, financial interests and the use and enjoyment of land. Negligence is the most relevant tort in today's society and you will see examples of it daily in newspapers and other media. Negligence is based on not taking enough care to ensure people are kept safe from harm. For example, a council could be liable for uneven pavements because it should take care to ensure residents are not harmed, so should fix the pavement or put up a sign. I am sure you have seen plenty of 'uneven pavement' signs. This is because the council wants to show it has taken sufficient care so cannot be successfully sued in court.

Example

A negligence claim was brought in the UK courts against McDonalds because the coffee was too hot and someone was scalded. The claim failed, but in 2017 a woman successfully sued Starbucks in America because she was badly scalded when the lid popped off her coffee. Even though the McDonalds claim failed, the same could happen here in the latter type of situation because more care should be taken. Although you would expect coffee to be hot, so should take care yourself when drinking it, you would not expect the lid to pop off. Starbucks should have taken more care to ensure the lids were safe.

The nature of law not only covers what law is and where it comes from, as well as the differences between civil and criminal law, but also includes how law operates in society, involving different theories (or concepts) of law. These concepts need to be related to all your other areas of study, so as well as explaining the particular concept; each chapter will provide examples from both criminal and civil law. Here is a brief overview as an introduction to the nature of law followed by an example and tasks. This should help you understand each concept when you come to study it in detail.

1.2 An introduction to the nature of law

Law and morality – as noted when looking at rules, the law only punishes someone for breaking legal rules, not social (or moral) ones. However, legal rules sometimes overlap with social rules and morality. This is what law and morality is about: how far social and legal rules overlap and whether the law should be involved in moral issues. Sometimes the law has to get involved because a moral issue comes up in court (examples are whether life support can be withdrawn from a patient in a coma and whether an anorexic teenager could be force-fed against her wishes).

Law and justice – justice is in the very nature of law and is similar to the rule of law (see below). Fairness and equality are part of the rule of law but are also the basis for justice, at least to most people. One view of justice (positivism) is that justice depends on legal rules. A law that is made properly using the correct procedures will be a valid law whether or not it is moral. Another view of justice (natural law) is that law is based on moral rules, so if a law is not moral it is not a true law. A third view is that justice does not need a moral content but is achieved where the most people get the most benefit from the law (called utilitarianism). This shows the overlap between justice and morality.

The rule of law is discussed below. This concept contains many of the elements required by justice and many cases could be used to illustrate both these concepts. For any area of study you should consider two questions:

- ***Is the legal system just (procedural justice)?***
- ***Is a particular law just (substantive justice)?***

Law and society: Fault – both civil and criminal liability is based (usually) on fault, or to put it another way a person is not liable unless blameworthy. Fault is an indicator of blame so it justifies the imposition of liability. The usual level of fault in tort is being negligent, not reaching the expected standard of someone in the same position and thereby causing another person harm or loss. In criminal law the level of fault varies and can be intention, recklessness, negligence and sometimes none at all.

Law and society: Balancing competing interests – the law must balance different interests (or rights) between individuals (private interests), and between an individual and the state or society (the public interest), to achieve justice. The law plays a role in society by way of social control. One method of controlling people's behaviour is to make laws regulating it. In doing this the law needs to balance competing interests, those of society and those of individuals within that society. There are many laws regulating behaviour that are civil rather than criminal matters. However, many can involve both types of law, such as health and safety regulations where a breach of the rules can lead to a civil claim for negligence and a criminal prosecution. The law also has to balance competing interests when dealing with disputes between the parties in a court case. This occurs in all cases but is particularly true of land-based torts which involve disputes between neighbours.

Law and technology – as technology develops and new technologies arrive the law must be prepared to keep up. Criminal examples are internet and email scams, online abuse and cyber-crime in general. Civil examples include advanced medical techniques which lead to disagreements as to whether a procedure is ethical. Technological advances can lead to new procedures which haven't been possible before, e.g., cloning and tissue typing, and may need the intervention of the law in the case of disputes. Other examples are the use of drones and driverless cars, or robot-controlled procedures. These may lead to cases of negligence but there is the question of who the claim will be against – you cannot sue a robot! Drones used for deliveries are already the subject of complaints from people who say they have been a nuisance and in October 2017 someone shot an Amazon delivery drone out of the air because he was so fed up with the noise. Other issues relate to data protection and privacy because these are harder to control with such easy access to information through the internet.

The best way to see how the concepts apply in practice is by relating them to a case example. Here is an example of how all these theories can apply in a given situation. It is not an area you will study as it was a rape case, but it is an interesting example not only of the concepts, but also the English legal system (sources of law and influences on Parliament).

Example

R v R 1991, involved a man accused of raping his wife. They were separated and she had moved back in with her parents. He forced his way in to their house and assaulted her while attempting rape. At the time, rape within marriage was not against the law because a woman was deemed to have consented to sex purely by being married. The case went to the House of Lords (now the Supreme Court) on appeal.

The HL decided that rape within marriage was no longer acceptable. Although this was not about law and technology, it is an example of the law needing to keeping up with change, in this case changing social attitudes. The judges presumably felt they achieved justice for the wife. Whether the man achieved justice is another matter. It is part of the concept of justice that the law is not retrospective and however wrong he may have been morally, at the time of the event his action was not against the law. In making the decision the court exercised a form of social control. In order to do this it had to balance the competing interests of D (not to be guilty of what had at the time been a legal act) against those of his wife (to have the law's protection) and the wider public interest (violence can affect society as a whole). The public interest will usually prevail and here there was the added interest of the wife. The fact that the act was accompanied by violence showed a greater degree of fault, which may have tipped the balance against D. He should be punished (sanctioned) for his wrongdoing and society should be controlled so that this type of behaviour is eradicated. Finally, there is clearly a moral issue because the judges thought the law was wrong to allow an immoral act such as rape, even within marriage. However, Hart (a positivist) could say the decision should be based only on legal rules not morality, and that D should not have been punished for what was at the time a legal action, even if it was immoral.

However, Devlin (a supporter of natural law) might agree that he should be punished because the law which allowed rape within marriage was itself immoral and so not valid.

It is also arguable that an elected Parliament should decide on whether this type of act is against the law, not unelected judges. In fact, Parliament did act, after the event, and changed the law to match the decision.

A utilitarian would say this decision, and the later law by Parliament, achieved justice as a greater number of people benefit from the law prohibiting acts of violence, especially as (unlike **Brown 1994**) it was against the victim's wishes.

These first two tasks give you an idea of how you might think about these concepts as you read a particular case, the first from crime, the second from tort.

Task 1

In **Brown 1994**, serious injuries had occurred during consensual sado-masochistic sex in private. This was a criminal case and those involved were convicted of grievous bodily harm. They were all adults and no-one was forced to participate, but the court decided that the defence of consent could not be applied to serious harm where it was intentional. One judge said that the public should be protected from violence and that society itself was harmed by such behaviour, even if it happened in private. Another judge said it was not for the courts to protect people from themselves.

Briefly explain how the nature of law played a role in this case (justice, morality and social control)

Task 2

In **Bolton v Stone 1951**, a woman was walking down a street near a cricket ground when she was hit and injured by a cricket ball. She sued the club and claimed compensation for her injuries. The court ruled that the club had not been negligent because they had erected a high fence and taken other precautions to try to prevent this happening and also sporting activities are a social benefit.

Do you think the decision achieved justice?

What was the role of law in society (and what competing interests were balanced)?

What role did morality play?

Another concept that is needed for all law courses, as it permeates every bit of law and the legal system, is the rule of law. This is sometimes covered with the English legal system but some examination boards include it with the nature of law so I have added it here with the other concepts.

When laws are formulated they should conform to the rule of law. This involves equality, clarity and fairness.

- ***The law should apply to everyone equally and no-one should be above the law.***
- ***The law must be clear so that people know the rules (then if the rules are broken it will be fair to punish those at fault).***
- ***The law must be accessible so that if a person is accused of a crime it is only fair that access to justice and legal advice is possible.***

This is a simplified description of the rule of law, but is a sound base when you are trying to connect the rule of law to a particular law or procedure. However, it needs further explanation.

1.3 The Rule of Law

The **Constitutional Reform Act 2005** refers to the rule of law, and the Lord Chancellor's oath requires the Lord Chancellor to respect the rule of law, but there is no agreed definition of it. An early view of the rule of law is that formulated by Dr Thomas Fuller in 1733: *"Be you ever so high, the law is above you"*. This view has continued for centuries. In **Evans v AG 2015**, the SC ruled that correspondence between Prince Charles and government ministers should be made public under the **Freedom of Information Act** and said it was *"fundamental to the rule of law"* that decisions and actions of the executive are subject to review in a court of law. The nature of the rule of law is that powers exercised by the state (politicians and public officials) are based on an authority that conforms to minimum standards of substantive or procedural justice. Thus the powers must have a legal foundation.

The rule of law was popularised by A. V. Dicey (a constitutional lawyer) the following century who, in summary, said *"everyone, whatever his rank, is subject to the ordinary law of the land"*. A little more recently, Lord Bingham said *"If you maltreat a penguin in the London zoo, you do not escape prosecution because you are the Archbishop of Canterbury"*. So, an important part of the rule of law is that everyone is subject to it, with no exclusions. There is more to it than that, and opinions differ on what it means in the modern sense. Although the rule of law is a somewhat abstract notion, to try to explain it today a good place to start is with Lord Bingham's 2014 lecture on the subject, taken from his book 'The Rule of Law'. The core principle is as above, that no-one is above the law, including those who make it. He notes that the rule of law has evolved and continues to do so, and sets out eight sub-rules which he feels describe the rule of law in its current form. These are:

Law must be accessible. This means that if people are bound by the law they must be able to know what the law is.

Questions of legal rights and liabilities should be resolved by application of the law and not be a matter of discretion. This does not mean there is absolutely no discretion. A judge must exercise a certain amount of discretion when deciding on an appropriate sentence or remedy – the point is that any such discretion is limited by law, e.g., statutes or earlier decisions.

The law should apply equally to all. This is accepted by most people as being part of any rule of law but Lord Bingham points out that in practice it is not always apparent. An example is the various **Terrorism Acts** where non-nationals suspected of terrorism are subject to being locked up without trial, but nationals are not – even though they pose the same threat. It is arguable that anyone subject to national laws should be entitled to the law's protection. Even where the law appears to apply equally it may not in practice. It is true that the Archbishop of Canterbury is not above the law – but if he does mistreat a penguin he can probably afford a decent lawyer to help his case! The **Legal Aid, Sentencing and Punishment of Offenders Act 2012 (LASPO)**, has severely reduced access to justice and legal aid, especially in civil cases.

The law should adequately protect fundamental human rights. This is perhaps a more recent addition to the concept of the rule of law. The preamble to the **Universal Declaration of Human Rights** says that if people are not to be compelled to rebel against tyranny and oppression that "human rights should be protected by the rule of law".

The state must meet its obligations under international law. Thus an act by a state that is unlawful would be against the rule of law. He referred to the war against Iraq and, whilst not saying whether or not he believed it to be illegal, he did say that if it *was* illegal then it would be against the rule of law "if this sub-rule is sound".

Means must be provided for resolving civil disputes. He says that if people are bound by the law they should receive its benefits and should be able to go to court to have their rights and liberties determined "in the last resort". He does not rule out less formal methods of resolving disputes but sees access to the courts as a "basic right" adding that legal advice should be affordable and available without excessive delay. Where the first sub-rule requires law to be accessible in the sense of clarity, this sub-rule requires accessibility in terms of cost. It has been said that justice is open to all "like the Ritz hotel" – meaning that everyone may be entitled to it but many are unable to use it in practice due to lack of money. Going back to the mistreatment of penguins, the Archbishop is more likely to be able to afford to go to the Ritz and to gain access to justice than the average person on the street is, especially since **LASPO**.

All public officials must exercise their power reasonably and not exceed its limits. As with the second rule, this rule is against the arbitrary use of power. An example of its application is that everyone has the right to apply for judicial review of a decision made by public officers and government ministers – a judge cannot overturn such a decision, but can rule that it is unreasonable.

Adjudicative procedures must be fair. This means open court hearings, the right to be heard, the right to know what the charges and evidence against you are, that the decision maker is independent and impartial, and that in criminal cases D is innocent until guilt is proved. Fairness would also cover access to justice in both the earlier senses of clarity and cost.

Lord Bingham sees the rule of law as depending on an unspoken bargain between the individual and the state. The citizen sacrifices some freedom by accepting legal constraints on certain activities, and the state sacrifices some power by recognising it cannot do all that it has the power to do. He concludes that this means those who maintain and protect the rule of law are "guardians of an all but sacred flame which animates and enlightens the society in which we live".

To sum up the rule of law:

No-one is above the law

Everyone is subject to the law, not the arbitrary exercise of power

The law must encompass clarity, access to justice, fairness and an independent and impartial judiciary

The law must apply equally

In Lord Bingham's view, the rule of law should also protect human rights and comply with international obligations if it is to apply to a modern state with national and international commitments. Bear that in mind if you will be studying human rights.

As you study the law try to consider whether the rule of law is being upheld.

Task 3

Explain what Lord Bingham meant when he said *"If you maltreat a penguin in the London zoo, you do not escape prosecution because you are the Archbishop of Canterbury"*. Add a comment of your own as to whether you agree that this should be part of the rule of law.

Evaluation pointer

An important role for the law is to uphold the rule of law. Another is to achieve justice. Both these require, among other things, equality, clarity and fairness. Any of the cases you see where the decision seems wrong on the facts, can illustrate a lack of fairness. Cases where there is inconsistency can illustrate a lack of clarity, and cases where those involved are not treated equally can illustrate a lack of equality. As you look at case examples bear this in mind. This will give you lots of material to illustrate a discussion of the nature of law in achieving justice, and will help you understand and explain how the rule of law applies.

Chapter 2 Law and Morals

'... there remains an area of private morality and immorality that is not the law's business'

The Wolfenden Report, 1957

By the end of this Chapter you should be able to:

- ***Distinguish between law and morals and recognise and illustrate the diversity of moral views***
- ***Identify opposing academic and judicial views on the relationship between law and morals***
- ***Explain how the law may be used to promote or enforce morality***
- ***Produce an argument for or against the law promoting/enforcing morality, using case examples***

2.1 What is morality

There is no strict definition of what amounts to 'morality' and no universal distinction between moral wrongs and legal ones.

Example

A common example used is that of a person walking past someone who is drowning and taking no action. Asked whether it is a crime not to try to save them, many students answer 'yes', but in the UK the answer is 'no'. There is usually no criminal liability for a failure to act, an omission. You might say, 'Well, you *should* try to save them.' This is a **moral** issue. You may have a **moral** duty to act but you have no **legal** duty to do so. As our law stands, it is left to the individual. This is a libertarian view of the law which is based on personal autonomy. This is what law and morals is all about; the question of how far the law *is*, and *should be*, imposing rules and how far any action should be left to individual choice.

A common view of morality is that it is a body of rules which govern a group's behaviour. This sounds a bit like law, too, so what is the difference? Well, to some people there isn't one, but to others the two concepts are separate.

We saw in the introduction that there are two broad approaches to the relationship between law and morals. The positivist approach sees law and morals as separate. The natural law view sees law and morals as linked. The first looks at what law is and if the law was created properly it is a true law. The second looks at what the law ought to be, so if a law is not moral it is not a true law. These are theories of justice so discussed further in the next chapter. Another theory is the libertarian one that upholds personal autonomy as paramount. Under this view people should be able to do as they choose unless the act could harm others.

Task 4

Consider whether the following are/should be illegal or immoral. If possible, ask a friend to do this too. See if you agree.

- ***Murder***
- ***Smoking in public***
- ***Cheating in examinations***
- ***Speeding***

- ***Swearing in public***
- ***Shoplifting***
- ***Adultery***
- ***Lying***
- ***Parking on a double yellow line***

Morality is a society's code of behaviour, the principles and standards by which we live. Law is a set of rules which regulates our activities within society. Both morals and law are based on regulating behaviour but there are differences.

2.2 The differences between moral and legal rules

Moral rules develop over time and don't change overnight. Law can be made relatively quickly by Parliament or the higher courts. It took a very long time for society to decide that rape within marriage was wrong and gay marriage was acceptable but the law on these issues then changed quite quickly, first in the HL and then by Parliament.

A moral code is usually willingly accepted by members of the society to which it applies. There is no need for formal sanctions for breaking the rules because they are enforced through social disapproval. Thus moral rules are voluntary, they ought to be obeyed but do not have to be. Law applies to everyone and must be obeyed.

Here is a comparison.

Moral rules	• Develop gradually over time and don't change overnight • *Should* be obeyed • Are enforced by the disapproval of friends, family and society • Are voluntary and apply to those who willingly accept them and agree to be bound by them
Legal rules	• Can change quickly by Acts of Parliament or court cases • *Must* be obeyed • Are enforced by legal sanctions through the courts • Are not voluntary and apply to everyone

Despite these differences, there is a significant overlap between morality and law as both are based on rules which govern our behaviour. However, there is much disagreement over how far they do, and should, overlap – I doubt you and your friend agreed on everything in the above task. There may be consensus on some issues, or at least a dominant view, but individuals within society will differ in what they regard as morally acceptable. Crimes such as murder, theft and rape are generally held to be both immoral and illegal. Traffic offences are crimes but not generally seen as immoral. However, even killing can be morally acceptable and some say should be legal in certain cases, such as euthanasia, and parking on a yellow line is arguably immoral if you are blocking an emergency exit.

Adultery, swearing and cheating are not illegal but may be viewed as immoral. Lying may be immoral, and is sometimes illegal, e.g., lying in court or in certain documents. Shoplifting is theft, but some would argue it isn't morally wrong to take a bone from a butcher's shop to feed a starving dog. The ban on smoking which came into force in 2007 under the **Health Act 2006** is an example of the overlap. Many argue that the law should not interfere; that it is a matter of individual choice or personal autonomy. Others argue that smoking can harm others, so should be illegal. Similar debates arose over the banning of foxhunting, which was purely a moral issue but is now illegal too.

The ban on smoking is an example of the law influencing the way society behaves. The law can also lead to a change in moral codes because it changes the way people think over time. When seat belts and crash helmets were made compulsory many people thought that it should be a matter of personal choice not law (the libertarian view, see under Mill below). The same thing happened with the law against driving with excess alcohol. These laws later became accepted so most people now see disobeying them as morally, as well as legally wrong. It may be that the same will happen with smoking and society will come to see it as morally wrong. At the moment society is still divided, but the law has already been extended.

Case example

The **Health Act 2006** was the subject of a judicial review in **R (on the application of Black) v the Secretary of State for Justice 2015**. The Act was not being applied in prisons, where smoking was still allowed in cells on the basis that this was 'home'. A prisoner claimed that the law was wrong to allow this and that secondary smoking affected his health. He argued that the Act should apply to prisons and the court agreed (although rejecting his argument that the policy breached his right to respect for private and family life under **Article 8 (A 8)** of the **European Convention on Human Rights (ECHR)**). However the CA allowed the government's appeal in recognition that a compulsory ban brought in suddenly could cause discipline and security problems, and the government should be allowed time to implement the non-smoking policy gradually. The government started pilot schemes in several prisons with the idea of phasing in the ban by the end of August 2017. This led to riots and prisoners argued that they should be allowed to smoke in their cells (as was the case) or at least outside in the yard. The ban came into force in 2017 but is still the subject of much debate. Health and safety come into both sides of the debate. Some say smoking should be illegal because it causes health problems. Others argue forcing people to give up has its own problems and there was evidence of severe depression and suicide in prisons where the pilot schemes took place. The law enforced morality by bringing in the **Health Act** and banning smoking but this did not apply equally, so arguably was against the rule of law. The law now enforces morality equally but opinion on whether it should is divided. This case highlights the problem of the law enforcing morality where views on what is moral differ.

In December 2017, the SC confirmed the decision that the **Health Act** did not bind the Crown, so Crown premises such as Her Majesty's Prisons did not have to enforce it. The SC used the purposive approach to interpretation, and held that if Parliament had intended the provisions to bind the Crown it would have made this clear.

2.3 Diversity of moral views

The less open a society the more likely there will be agreement on moral standards. The more freedom people have to express their views, the more likely it is that those views will differ.

The sociologist Emile Durkheim (1858-1917) saw the law as a means of ensuring that social structures worked. However, he noted that social change had led to the fragmentation of society and a diversity of moral views. If there is no agreement on what is morally acceptable, there is no single moral standard that can be applied when making or enforcing law.

As with fox hunting and smoking, what some people see as immoral, others don't. What is regarded as immoral in one society, or in one time, may not be so in another. We live in a plural society with diverse views as Durkheim pointed out, so there is no 'shared morality'. Adultery and abortion are other examples of differing opinions. These are legal in the UK but some believe them to be immoral, and in some countries they are crimes. Even giving advice on contraception in order to avoid an unwanted pregnancy has been the subject of legal challenge. In **Gillick v West Norfolk and Wisbech AHA 1986**, a mother challenged her daughter's doctor for prescribing contraceptives. She lost at first instance, won in the Court of Appeal (CA) and lost again in the HL by a majority of 3-2. There is no shared morality in the courts either, it seems. The case became famous and led to children having greater rights to make their own decisions on such matters as medical treatment, as long as they are what is now called 'Gillick competent'.

In **Axon v Secretary of State for Health 2006**, a mother argued that the Gillick principle conflicted with **Article 8** of the **European Convention on Human Rights (ECHR)**, the right to a private and family life. She said that parents had a right to be informed about children seeking advice or treatment on sexual issues. The CA held that parental rights reduce as the child gets older and more knowledgeable. Confirming the principle of 'Gillick competence', the CA held that the right to be informed ceases to exist once the child is competent to make his or her own decisions. This illustrates that the law may need to be involved in moral issues to protect young children, but also recognises that as the child gets older the decision should be left to the individual concerned. An example is collective worship in schools. **S 70** of the **School Standards and Framework Act 1998** provides that all state maintained schools must have daily collective worship which must be "wholly or mainly of a broadly Christian character". Parents can ask for a child to be excused but a child cannot opt out until the sixth form (or of school-leaving age). This is an example of the problem of enforcing moral values when there is no shared morality, as Durkheim recognised. The law on collective worship can be divisive, especially where a school has an ethnic mix of pupils. Although parents can ask for their child to be excused, most don't because they don't want to alienate their child from other pupils.

Schools can apply to the local authority for exemption from the "broadly Christian" requirement for some or all of their pupils. This is called a "determination", and alternative worship must be provided for the exempted pupils. This avoids enforcing moral Christian values on all school children, but again has the problem of being divisive and segregating the children instead of integrating them. On a similar issue, an Islamic school which insisted on segregation of the sexes was held to be in breach of the **Equality Act 2010**. In October 2017, the CA held that despite the fact that the **School Standards and Framework Act** allowed for parental choice, this could not negate the right of all children to be educated in a non-discriminatory way.

The law needs to keep up with changes in technology as well as social views. Advances in medical technology led to the setting up of the **Warnock Committee**. This looked at several issues involving in-vitro fertilisation (IVF), including the use of embryos in medical research. It reported in 1984 and many of its findings were included in the **Human Fertilisation and Embryology Act 1990** (as amended by the **HFE 2008**). As noted above, both law and morals involve rules. The courts enforce the law, but not social rules. However, if the morality is shared then most people will obey the rules. The question is should moral issues be a matter for society alone, or should the law promote and/or enforce morality? The problem with making social rules into legal ones is the conflict of opinion about most moral issues. If morality is not shared then *whose* values should the law reflect when promoting or enforcing morals? The difficulties were recognised at the time of the Committee report. Mary Warnock, the academic who chaired the committee, made this point:

"I do not believe there is a neat way of marking off moral issues from all others; some people, at some time, may regard things as matters of moral right and moral wrong, which at another time or in another place are thought to be matters of taste, or of no importance at all."

Task 5

Social rules can be enforced by society's disapproval of any breach of the rules. Jumping the queue at the supermarket checkout to get your shopping home earlier isn't illegal but few of us do it because we know our behaviour will be disapproved of.

Legal rules are enforced by the police and the courts. Jumping the traffic lights to get your shopping home earlier *is* illegal and we don't do it because it is against the law and we will be punished.

Imagine you are with a group of people stranded on a desert island. You need to make some rules to govern behaviour. Make a list of six rules you think are important. Now go on to decide if they should have the force of law. How will they be enforced?

Examination tip

Read the question carefully. You may be asked how far the law *promotes* moral values, if so discuss laws which actively seek to make society behave in a certain way. Examples would be the **Health Act** prohibiting smoking, the **Hunting Act** prohibiting fox hunting and the **Racial and Religious Hatred Act** prohibiting the incitement of hatred due to someone's race or religion. These laws aim to promote morality by providing new rules to engineer how people behave. The law comes first and promotes the changing of society's moral code.

If asked how far the law *enforces* moral values then discuss laws which *reflect* society's views. Criminal case examples include **R v R 1991** and **Brown 1994** (see Chapter 1). In civil law the case of **Donoghue v Stevenson 1932** promoted the taking of greater care to avoid harming other people. The **Consumer Protection Act** and **Consumer Rights Act** then extended the enforcement of the duty of care. These laws aim to enforce morality by stating that certain behaviour (rape, serious harm and poor standards of care) is not acceptable and should be punished. Here the moral code comes first and the law follows and enforces that code.

In 2004, a Russian newspaper carried a report that Moscow city authorities were considering a ban on kissing and embracing on the underground. The *Stolichnaya Vechernaya* said the ban, aimed at raising public morality, could even extend to a husband embracing his wife. This may be a Russian case, but it is a clear example of a government promoting moral values *via* the law.

2.4 The relationship between law and morals

The relationship between law and morality is complex and questions arise as to whether one is shaped by the other. If so, which shapes which – and which *should* shape which? Does the law decide what is 'moral' or does society's view of morality shape the law?

One major report about the law and how far it should reflect morality is the **Wolfenden Committee Report 1957** on homosexuality and prostitution. This may have been some time ago but it is a useful starting point when looking at the relationship between law and morals. The report noted that the purposes of the criminal law are:

"... to preserve public order and decency, to protect the citizen from what is offensive and injurious and to provide sufficient safeguards against exploitation and corruption of others especially the vulnerable ... The law should not intervene in the private lives of citizens or seek to enforce any particular pattern of behaviour further than necessary to carry out the above purposes."

The opening quote came from this report. The committee recommended that prostitution and homosexual acts between consenting adult males in private should no longer be criminal offences. However, activities associated with prostitution, which could cause offence to others (such as soliciting in the street), were still to be regulated by the law.

The **Wolfenden Report** became the subject of a major legal debate between **Lord Devlin**, a judge who took the view that law and morality are inextricably linked, and **Professor Hart**, an academic who argued that there is no widely shared morality (see also the Chapter on Justice).

The Hart-Devlin debate

View 1 – law and morality are separate (the positivist view)

Hart argued that using the law to enforce morality was unnecessary, undesirable and morally unacceptable.

Unnecessary because society would not otherwise disintegrate

Undesirable because it would freeze morality at that time

Unacceptable because it would restrict the freedom of the individual

Hart was heavily influenced by John Stuart Mill (see the philosopher's view below), and he approved of the commission's approach to liberalising the laws to allow greater personal autonomy. He did not think the law should regulate behaviour unless it caused harm. Hart was more paternalistic than Mill and included harm to oneself in this, so would expect the law to criminalise euthanasia.

A case where the law refused to enforce morality was **R (on the application of Green) v City of Westminster Magistrates' Court 2007**. The group Christian Voice argued that the play 'Jerry Springer: the Opera' was a blasphemous libel and so an offence at common law. The court held that for this offence there not only had to be an attack on Christianity in some way but it also had to 'endanger society' by 'depraving public morality' or causing civil strife. The court found that, as regards the second element, the play had been showing in London for two years without any such effect on society. Blasphemy laws have been criticised as biased and unclear and were abolished in 2008. The **Racial and Religious Hatred Act 2006** covers some of the matters that previously came under blasphemy laws but applies to all religions not just Christianity. The **Act** is an example of the law attempting to engineer the way society behaves, as with the **Health Act**.

View 2 – law and morality are linked (the natural law view)

Lord **Devlin** was vehemently against Hart's viewpoint. He argued that immoral acts, even in private, could weaken the fabric of society. He would therefore want euthanasia regulated by the criminal law even though a private act. Devlin thought that society should punish an act thought grossly offensive and immoral by the standards of the 'right-minded person'. He would therefore want immoral acts regulated by the criminal law even if they occurred in private. The problem is identifying the content of this morality and deciding who Devlin's right-minded people are.

Two older cases illustrate support for Lord Devlin's view. In **Shaw v DPP 1961,** arguments for upholding a conviction for 'conspiring to corrupt public morals' (by publishing a directory of prostitutes) rested on the need to *"conserve the moral welfare of the state"*. In **Knuller v DPP 1973 HL,** the court convicted the Ds for publishing advertisements for homosexuals. Although the **Sexual Offences Act 1967** had made homosexuality legal following the Wolfenden Report, Lord Reid said

"... if people choose to corrupt themselves in this way that is their affair and the law will not interfere. But no licence is given to others to encourage this practice."

The same applies to prostitution. This is not illegal, but people who make money from the practice, such as brothel keepers and pimps, are committing an offence. Even though the Wolfenden Committee recommended that homosexuality and prostitution be legalised, the report made clear that one of the functions of the law is to provide safeguards against the exploitation and corruption of others, and this view is reflected in the laws which followed the report.

A couple having sex in a Domino's Pizza take-away was the subject of a case in 2017 where the law enforced morality. The couple's actions were caught on CCTV and the footage was released on social media. They were convicted of the common law offence of outraging public decency. Although the magistrates noted that there was no identifiable victim, they said that harm caused was to the public, which was outraged. The problem with this is that it is the magistrates and judges who decide whether the public is outraged. There appeared to be little evidence to support this view at the trial.

The philosopher's view (the libertarian view)

The philosopher **John Stuart Mill (1806 – 1873)**, of whom more in the next chapter on Law and Justice, would have agreed with the Committee. His view was that the principle of personal autonomy was important and the law should leave people to make their own choices, so long as they do not harm others. Many lawyers and judges have been influenced by this view. It can be argued, however, that there are very few actions that have no effect on others. Look back to the smoking argument. The law on euthanasia has often been challenged and there are strong opposing views on this issue of law and morals. It is unclear how Mill would view it. The principle of personal autonomy would probably be paramount in cases where the person concerned is able to make a clear choice. However, the harm to others principle could come into play if that was not the case. Euthanasia is discussed in detail under 'Morality and the criminal law' as it illustrates several opposing views on morality and there are plenty of cases on it too.

The case of **R (on the application of Green) v City of Westminster Magistrates' Court 2007**, above, accords with Mill's view, as freedom of expression was upheld on the basis that the public were not harmed. Devlin might have disagreed because he thought morality was an essential part of society, so restricting personal freedom was justified if it safeguarded morality. To sum up:

- Devlin's view is that the law should interfere in personal freedom to protect society. If the conduct is wrong, the law should forbid it.
- Mill's view is that the law should only interfere in personal freedom to protect other people from harm. The law should not intervene because the conduct is wrong, but because it is harmful.
- Hart's view is that the law should only interfere in personal freedom to protect people from harm but extends Mill's harm principle to harming oneself.

There are therefore conflicting views on how far the law should enforce moral values and this can be seen in the **Brown** case.

The judges' view: The Brown Case

In **Brown 1994**, the HL held that, where the Ds had committed homosexual sadomasochistic acts, resulting in injuries, public policy demanded that these acts be treated as unlawful even though they occurred in private and the participants had consented. There was not only disagreement in the decision (a 3-2 majority), but in the reasoning behind it showing a diversity of views among the Law Lords.

Lord Templeman said, *"Society is entitled and bound to protect itself against a cult of violence. Pleasure derived from the infliction of pain is an evil thing"*.

Lord Lowry said such activities were not *"conducive to the welfare of society"*. Both these views accord with Devlin's. However, the two dissenting judges were more in line with Hart, that law and morality were not inextricably linked. Lord Mustill took the view that although the acts were immoral that did not make them unlawful and the conviction should be quashed. Lord Slynn said it was not for the courts to protect people from themselves.

N.B.: The European Court of Human Rights upheld the majority view in ***Brown*** *and held that the conviction and imprisonment of the offenders did not violate the right to respect for private life under Article 8 of the European Convention on Human Rights.*

The fact that the decision was influenced by the judges' views of what was morally acceptable can be seen by comparing it to **Wilson 1996,** where D was acquitted after branding his initials on his wife's buttocks.

Task 6

Do you think Mill would have approved of the ban on smoking or not?

What do you think Mill's view would have been had he been a judge in **Brown**?

Evaluation pointer

It can be argued that judges are not the right people to decide issues of morality. If these issues are not to be left to individual choice, should it be for Parliament alone to lay down the law? In **Gibson 1991**, an artist exhibited earrings made from freeze-dried foetuses. He was convicted of outraging public decency. As with the couple having sex in a pizza take-away, society may be 'outraged' but has it been harmed? Although natural law may approve of such decisions, Mill would probably argue that the law should not interfere.

2.5 Legal enforcement of morality

We have seen that there are diverse views on morality, looked at the relationship between law and morals and touched on how far the law enforces morals. We now need to look at the enforcement of morality in connection with different areas of law and to consider how far the law should enforce morality. Some will argue that the law should enforce morality as the protector of society. This is seen in the words of Lord Templeman and Lord Lowry in **Brown**. Others will argue that the law should not interfere in moral issues and should leave it to individual choice. This is seen in the views of the two dissenting judges in the same case. Euthanasia and assisted suicide illustrate similar conflicts, with the principle of the sanctity of life (Devlin) in conflict with the principle of personal autonomy (Hart/Mill).

One argument for keeping morals and law separate is the problem with who is making the law. Parliament is better able to take time to debate the issue and is democratically elected. However, politicians are reluctant to pass controversial laws that may cost them votes when it comes to election time. Judges can base their decisions on the law but may be influenced by morality as seen in **Brown**. The judiciary may be a little more diverse than it was but it is still acknowledged that judges tend to come from a narrow social background (and are not elected). These points support the argument that the law should not involve itself in morality.

So how far do the courts and Parliament enforce morality?

A contemporary issue that can illustrate the relationship between law and morals is 'designer babies', so-called because during IVF treatment choices can be made. The HL ruled in **Attorney-General's Reference (No 3 of 1994) 1997**, that a foetus is not a *"reasonable creature in being"*. An embryo is therefore not a human being for the purposes of a murder charge. However, there is much debate about whether or not people should be able to choose the genetic make-up of their babies. Choosing an embryo means discarding other embryos. Many argue this is immoral, and should be illegal. Most would agree that this should not be done for social reasons, e.g., to balance the number of boys and girls in a family, but where there are medical reasons it is perhaps more acceptable.

This moral question raises legal issues. It was the subject of **Quintavalle v Human Fertilisation and Embryology Authority 2005**. A couple had been granted the right by the Authority to use 'tissue typing' to select an embryo that would be a match for their son who was seriously ill and needed a transplant. This would mean an embryo that was not a match would be discarded. The pressure group CORE (Comment on Reprographic Ethics) challenged the Authority's right to do so under the **Human Fertilisation and Embryology Act 1990**. They argued that it could lead to people being able to have embryos tested (and discarded) for other characteristics, such as sex or hair colour – hence the term 'designer babies'. The HL, whilst recognising the case raised *"profound ethical questions"*, ruled that the **Act** could be interpreted as allowing selection. In August 2005, the government issued a consultation paper to assess public opinion on these issues. This resulted in the **Human Fertilisation and Embryology Act 2008** which was brought into effect over 2009/2010 and amends the **1990 Act**. Tissue typing can be licensed under the later **Act** where a sibling suffers from a serious medical condition, putting the decision in **Quintavalle** into statutory form. Also, although sex selection on social grounds is prohibited, the **Act** allows it if serious harm could otherwise occur, e.g., through a gender-related hereditary disease. This clarifies the earlier law and brings it up to date with medical advances – at least for the moment. This is an example of a moral issue being put into an Act of Parliament, which is arguably better than relying on interpretation by the courts on such a controversial subject.

There is still much debate on the subject and opinion is divided on advanced IVF technology and the creation of 'designer babies'. In 2013 it became possible to 'create' a child using the DNA from three people so as to avoid inheriting diseases. Some hailed it as a scientific breakthrough in the battle against killer diseases that were passed down through the generations; others saw it as producing three-parent families that were aberrant and went against nature.

The following examples illustrate the connection between law and morality in various areas of law and procedure from your course. AQA students should bear in mind that law and morals is assigned to Papers 2 and 3 and not Paper 1. However, AQA have confirmed that you can use any areas of law to help to explain the concepts as long as you focus on any specific points raised by the question. This means you can use the criminal case examples but may need also to discuss a specific tort or human right.

Examination tip

In an examination it is a good idea to use your own choice of examples. I have included a lot here so pick the ones that make most sense to you. You will produce a better essay if you use cases you know well and can discuss with confidence.

When discussing law and morality and how far they do, and should, overlap, note that your argument is not about right and wrong, but whether the matter should be classed as a legal issue or a matter of personal choice.

2.6 Morality and the criminal law

Criminal law has plenty of examples because many crimes have a moral element, especially offences against the person. The natural law view respects the sanctity of life so any murder or manslaughter cases can illustrate the law enforcing morality.

Failing to save a life may be immoral but not usually illegal. However, in cases such as **Stone & Dobinson** and **Gibbins & Proctor** there was a duty to act and so criminal liability arose. Other cases on omissions and a duty to act can be used to illustrate the relationship between law and morals. The case of **Khan 1998**, illustrates the law reflecting moral views as the men were found not to owe a duty to a young prostitute. It is arguable that leaving someone to die in those circumstances could be manslaughter, but this was not the case.

Killing is usually seen as both morally and legally wrong, but the relationship between law and morals in euthanasia and assisted suicide cases is not so clear. In some situations, the law appears to be enforcing morality and in others it does not.

All cases of euthanasia are potential murder cases because they involve an intention to kill. Whether they are treated as murder, assisted suicide or a legitimate ending of life will depend on the judges hearing the case and their views of the relationship between law and morals. The issue demonstrates the diversity of moral views and the different legal theories. It illustrates the natural law view that life is sacred and that the law should act to preserve life and enforce this morality. It also illustrates Mill's view that individuals should be allowed personal autonomy, as long as their actions do not harm others, and Hart's more paternalistic view that extends this to harm to oneself. The question is whether the issue is a matter for the individual or the state. It is significant in human rights law and a lot of these cases come under **Article 2** (the right to life) and / or **Article 8** (the right to respect for a private and family life). I have therefore put most of the case examples under that section, but here are a few arguments on the issue.

Writing in the New Law Journal following **Conway**, David Lawson said *"The first issue is whether this is a matter for the courts at all. Parliament has looked at assisted suicide at least 14 times since 2000 and is more likely than the courts to represent the full spectrum of views on the underlying ethical question"*.

In its 2004 report 'Partial Defences to Murder' the Law Commission said:

"the Government should undertake a public consultation on whether, and if so to what extent, the law should recognise either an offence of "mercy" killing or a partial defence of "mercy" killing".

In the **Falconer Report in 2011** the Commission on Assisted Dying proposed that euthanasia should be legalised subject to strict conditions. However, the emotive nature of the issue and the heated public debates mean it is unlikely that euthanasia will be made legal in England any time soon.

There is a fine line between assisted suicide and murder. This can be illustrated by comparing **Inglis 2010** and **Gilderdale 2010** discussed below. Both mothers had ended their severely disabled children's lives for similar reasons. In **Inglis** her son was unable to convey his wishes so it could not be classed as assisted suicide, the conviction was for murder. In **Gilderdale** her daughter had made her views clear and wanted to die, so the conviction was for assisted suicide. This has made it a difficult moral issue.

These cases clearly illustrate the problem with the law as it stands. The facts were similar but the first case was murder and resulted in a life sentence. The second was assisted suicide and resulted in a 12-month conditional discharge. The rule of law requires consistency and equality within the law, and so does justice. It can be argued that the law is failing on both these counts. **Gazeley 2015** is an example of the overlap. A man killed his wife at her request and after a loving marriage of thirty-five years and was charged with murder. The court refused to accept his argument that it was assisted suicide and he then pleaded diminished responsibility as a defence to murder. This was accepted and he was given a two year suspended sentenced for manslaughter.

Even if not made legal in the UK, if euthanasia was made a partial defence along with diminished responsibility and loss of control, this would allow for discretion in sentencing and perhaps make juries more willing to convict. If killing is immoral then it is also immoral that someone should be acquitted because the jury are reluctant to see him or her get a life sentence.

One form of euthanasia has seen a limited move to legality, and that is the withdrawal of life support. In **Bland 1993**, doctors had to make a moral decision to end the life of a boy in a permanent coma, but needed the court to confirm there would be no legal repercussions. This is because this could be classed as murder (the intention is clearly to end someone's life). The HL allowed the withdrawal of treatment. This is a type of passive euthanasia but critics see it as more immoral than active euthanasia, such as giving a lethal injection. This is because the process is long drawn out as the person is dehydrated over a period of time which leads to kidney failure and death. In the CA Lord Hoffman had recognised the principle of the sanctity of life but said it should not be taken to the point where it is empty of meaning and sacrifices "*other important values such as human dignity and freedom of choice*". The courts have made clear in many later cases that the decision does not apply to positive acts, as seen in **Cox 1992**.

In **Re M 2011**, the court held it was not in the patient's best interests to withdraw artificial feeding, even though the family wanted this, because the coma was not as deep as it was in **Bland**. The preservation of life was the deciding factor in the case, an example of the law reflecting morality.

In what has been called a landmark ruling the High Court has now stated that cases like **Bland** should not need to go to court and that it should be a matter for the doctors not the judges to decide. The case was **M v A Hospital 2017** and involved a woman who was terminally ill and whose mother supported her desire to have life support withdrawn. The judge said there was a strong presumption that it is in a person's best interests to stay alive but that "*this is not an absolute, and there are cases where it will not be in the patient's interests to receive life-sustaining treatment*". This case can be used to illustrate the law not enforcing morality. However, it would go against the natural law view, as would the next example.

In **Re A (conjoined twins) 2000**, an operation to separate conjoined twins (Mary and Jodie) would lead to the death of Mary. Legally, this could be murder as the doctors would have intent to kill Mary, which is why the case went to court for an order that the operation could go ahead. Morally, this would be against the natural law view that life is sacred and must be preserved. However, without the operation both twins would die, so it could be argued that Mary's death was justified to save Jodie's life. This is a utilitarian view of justice (see Chapter 3). Utilitarianism requires the law to bring about the 'greatest good', which would be life for at least one of the two twins. The HL allowed the operation. Ward LJ said *"Everyone seems to have a view of the proper outcome. I am very well aware of the inevitability that our answer will be applauded by some but that as many will be offended by it"*. This illustrates the diversity of moral views and the difficulties the law faces when dealing with such cases.

Task 7

Choose two criminal cases and make some notes on the moral issues involved. Then add your view of whether the matter should have been a question of law or left to individual choice.

Abortion in the UK is legal but some see it as immoral and equivalent to murder. The law allows medical practitioners who have conscientious objections to abortion to refuse to participate in the process. In **Greater Glasgow and Clyde Health Board v Doogan 2014**, two midwives took their hospital to court because they had been required to take part in some administrative procedures involving patients terminating pregnancies. The SC took a purposive approach to interpreting the **Abortion Act 1967**, and held that the phrase *"to take part in any treatment authorised by the Act"* did not extend the right to refuse to participate to anything other than treatment. It did not include purely administrative matters such as booking in patients and assigning (other) midwives to them. The law had decided not to enforce morality.

For the non-fatal offences against the person **Brown 1994** is an obvious example of enforcing morality. Devlin would agree with the decision in **Brown**, and argue that the law needed to step in to protect society against evil. Hart and Mill would say it is not the law's place to enforce moral values. **Wilson 1996** can be used in comparison; did the judges decide differently on moral grounds?

The rules on the defences of insanity and automatism recognise that the law should not punish someone who does not know they are doing wrong. On the other hand, the limitations on the intoxication defence reflect society's view that drinking should not excuse criminal activity. The defence of consent has been discussed above. It was refused in **Brown 1994** but allowed in **Wilson 1996** on what seemed to be moral rather than legal grounds. Consent is not accepted as a defence to murder but there have been challenges to this in cases where people are too severely disabled to take their own lives and wish a doctor or family member to assist, as in **Pretty**. As discussed above, this is a difficult moral question.

As for property offences, theft can be related to the argument that stealing from the rich and giving to the poor is not immoral, although it is certainly illegal. Similarly, taking food to feed a starving child is morally acceptable. It can be argued that the **Ghosh** test is insufficiently clear and juries are inconsistent in applying it, so cannot achieve justice. A decision may be reached on moral grounds rather than legal ones if there seems to be justification for the theft. In many cases of criminal damage caused during protest campaigns the protesters have tried to use the defence that they have a moral right to protect property from, e.g., nuclear power or GM crops. However, this defence has so far failed. In **DPP v Blake 1993**, a vicar wrote biblical quotations on a wall outside Parliament and claimed that he had God's consent to cause criminal damage. He also failed. In these cases, moral arguments have been subjugated to legal rules. Some defences have a moral element as the law recognises that there may be some justification for committing the crime. However, in **Windle 1952** Lord Goddard said *"it would be an unfortunate thing if it were left to juries to consider whether some particular act was morally right or wrong. The test* [for the defence of insanity] *must be whether it is contrary to law ..."*. This would accord with the positivist view of the separation of law and morals.

2.7 Morality and contract law

Although contract is an area with fewer moral issues, there are still examples to be found. The law does not get involved if someone breaks a promise in most circumstances, as this is seen as purely a moral issue. However if the promise is made in court under oath it will do so. The law will also get involved where the promise is made in a legally binding contract. Contract is based on the exchange of promises and the law will impose sanctions on those who break their promises, as in **Ruxley Electronics 1996**, where D was awarded damages for breach of the term regarding the depth of the swimming pool. Generally, though, the courts are reluctant to interfere in the making of contracts based on 'freedom of contract'. This is in accord with Mill's argument that the law should not interfere unless harm will result. This can include economic harm so you could discuss the way both Parliament and the courts *will* interfere to protect the weaker party in consumer contracts, e.g., by imposing terms (**The Moorcock**) and by limiting the ability of a business to exclude liability or impose unfair terms (**CRA 2015**). The courts will also interfere where an agreement is the result of misrepresentation, duress or fraud.

2.8 Morality and the law of tort

Donoghue v Stevenson 1932 shows the courts are prepared to develop the law to protect a weaker party who has suffered harm. A moral link can be seen in the biblical idea of 'love thy neighbour' which Lord Atkin developed to 'do not harm your neighbour'. The policy part of the test from **Caparo 1990** allows the judge a great deal of flexibility as a duty will only be imposed if it is fair, just and reasonable to do so. This means that whether a duty is owed may be based partly on moral values. The court may look at what is best for society as a whole and/or may restrict the duty to avoid opening the floodgates to claims, especially where these would be paid by public funds. It is arguably immoral to pay compensation when the money was intended to provide health care or police protection. In **Hill v CC of West Yorkshire 1988** the police did not owe a duty because it was not in the interests of society. The HL held that the imposition of a duty might make the police less efficient in carrying out their duty, part of which is to protect the public. However, it can be said to be immoral that someone injured through the negligence of the police is not able to get compensation. The case of **Michael v CC of South Wales 2015** is more controversial because the victim had been in contact with the police so had greater proximity. Harm was also foreseeable because the police knew of the danger. However, the court decided the police still did not owe a duty, although two judges dissented. It can be argued that the dissenting judges were right and in these circumstances a duty should have been owed. Other cases that can be discussed in this context are those involving hospitals and local councils where any compensation would also come from public funds. Many such cases involve principles and a matter of principle usually has a moral base. A supporter of natural law could say that in principle it is wrong to put too much of a burden on the police, health authorities and other public services. It Is morally wrong and the law should reflect morality.

In **White 1999,** the police were unable to succeed in a claim for psychiatric harm, in part because it would be immoral to allow the police to get compensation but not the victims' families. In **Greatorex 2000,** the court thought it morally undesirable to allow members of a family to sue each other.

In **BRB v Herrington 1972,** the HL held BR owed a *"common duty of humanity"* to a child trespasser and later, Parliament reflected and enforced this morality by passing the **Occupiers' Liability Act 1984**. Other cases in this area show that the law is more likely to enforce morality when it comes to children. The council owed a duty in **Glasgow Corporation v Taylor 1922** and in **Jolley 2000** because it was right that the children were compensated and the court ruled that the councils should have taken greater care. The law stops enforcing morality in this way as the child gets older and so less care is expected of the occupier, as in **Tomlinson 2003** and **Poppleton 2008**. The law also recognises that a parent should be responsible for young children and it would be wrong to impose a duty on an occupier for an unaccompanied young child, as in **Phipps v Rochester Corporation 1955**.

Evaluation pointer

Should the law reflect and enforce morality? This depends on your view of law and the purposes it serves in society. Whether judges (rather than Parliament) should develop the law to enforce morality is another question. It is argued that judges are appointed rather than elected and not accountable to the people, so should not attempt to impose their views on others. On the other hand, it can be argued that they are independent, more objective and don't have to give way to popular opinion or keep the electorate happy. Development of the law can involve judges in questions of morality. This is arguably the role of Parliament where the issues can be fully debated. In **Quintavalle**, the pressure group CORE said the decision was *"certainly a defeat for parliamentary democracy."*

2.9 Morality and human rights

In **Gillick** and **Axon**, the court felt that individual choice was more important than enforcing a moral standard on the girls. In the latter case the court held that the principle of 'Gillick competence' did not breach **Article 8** of the **European Convention on Human Rights** (**ECHR**) on family life. **A 8** provides for the right to respect for a private and family life. This is in conflict with **A 10** which provides for freedom of expression. An example is **Murray v Express Newspapers 2008**, where the author of the Harry Potter books successfully fought against the publication of photographs of her son to protect his privacy. There are many other examples of the conflict between people trying to protect their privacy and others trying to tell stories about them in the media. These include cases involving Naomi Campbell, Michael Douglas and Rio Ferdinand (see Chapter 5 for more details). Keep an eye out in the media for current examples and see under 'technology' below for examples of the conflict between data collection and privacy under **A 8**.

Most of the assisted dying and euthanasia cases involve human rights as **Article 2** protects the right to life. Many cases are brought under **A 8** which is the right to respect for a private and family life which is wider. Both these rights are essentially moral issues where the law needs to balance the different interests.

There have been many cases challenging the law prohibiting assisted suicide, which is illegal under **s 2 Suicide Act 1961**. However, judges have been reluctant to go against the principle of the sanctity of life where there is a positive act such as helping someone to kill themselves. An early challenge was a judicial review case, **R (on the application of Pretty) v DPP 2002**. Mrs Pretty had tried to get immunity from prosecution for her husband if he helped her to die but her arguments failed to persuade the HL which held that the blanket ban on assisted suicide was a proportionate way to protect the weak and the vulnerable. In another judicial review case, **R (on the application of Purdy) v DPP 2009**, Mrs Purdy argued that the law on assisted suicide as it stands is unclear and unfair. The CA relied on **Pretty** and noted that as that was a decision of the HL it must be followed as a binding precedent. However, on appeal the Law Lords were unanimous in deciding that the DPP should issue clearer guidance on the criteria used when deciding whether to prosecute in cases of assisted suicide. The decision reflects the changing opinion of society in general on suicide, and on whether those who help someone to commit suicide should be prosecuted. However, although guidelines were published in 2010, the DPP said at the time *"The policy does not change the law on assisted suicide. It does not open the door for euthanasia"* and that each case has to be considered on its own facts and merits. This is not sufficiently reassuring for the person who wants to die, or for their partners, as it is so vague. Although there have so far not been any prosecutions since the guidelines were issued, the law has not changed. There is still the uncertainty of not knowing if you will be prosecuted if you help a loved one to die.

In **Pretty v UK** Mrs Pretty petitioned the ECtHR which confirmed that **A 2** did not extend to the right to die. She also claimed interference with her right to respect for a private and family life under **A 8**. This is wider and the ECtHR considered there was a possible interference. However, it concluded the law was deemed necessary in a democratic society and justified to protect the vulnerable.

Between these two cases, there was a slightly more unusual one. In **Burke v GMC 2006**, a man took a case to the ECtHR not arguing the right to die, but the right to life under **A 2**. He was seriously ill and feared treatment could be withdrawn against his wishes. The court held that it was for doctors to decide in the particular circumstances of the individual case. This case and that of **Bland** highlight the difficulties where the person is in a coma and cannot express an opinion. There is arguably stronger support for the natural law view of justice here because the law should protect people from harm. There have also been occasions, albeit rare, where people have recovered against all expectations after years in a deep coma. The law on assisted suicide is less defensible because the principle of personal autonomy should be paramount where people are able to make their wishes clear. In an email debate between Ms Purdy and another sufferer of the same disease the other sufferer was against the law changing to allow assisted suicide and said *"Assisting or encouraging someone to take their own life should not be enshrined in law."* His argument was that the law should protect the vulnerable and not be used to legalise any type of killing. This is a valid point and illustrates the difficulties the law faces.

In **Nicklinson & Another 2013**, Mr Nicklinson wanted his doctor to end his life but the guidelines do not extend to doctors, only family. Following the refusal of the court to make an order allowing the doctor's assistance, he started to refuse food and effectively starved himself to death. After he died the others appealed. The CA agreed the guidelines lacked clarity on the position if the person who assisted were not closely connected to the victim but said any change to the law should be left to Parliament. The SC said *"the issue involves a choice between two fundamental but mutually inconsistent moral values, the sanctity of life and the principle of autonomy"* and noted that there was *"no consensus in our society"*.

The principle of personal autonomy (the right to make one's own choices on life and death) needs to be balanced against the wider view, which would take in the fact that euthanasia affects society as a whole. Even without a moral content (the positivist view), it may be necessary for the law to balance the welfare of the individual against the welfare of society. This is the utilitarian view of justice, that the law should benefit the greatest number. Taking a life, even if it is your own or that of a loved one, is a serious matter. Therefore, it is not only a proponent of natural law who will argue that it should be against the law. If society itself is harmed by assisted suicide and euthanasia the greatest good is achieved by making it illegal, even if that would infringe the rights of some individuals. However a positivist like Hart would argue that the law should not be used to enforce morality because it would restrict individual choice. He was also concerned that it would mean that the law would reflect the moral values of that time and so would prevent change. These are serious and complex issues, perhaps better debated by Parliament than decided in a court of law. However, people affected by the law as it is have challenged it and someone has to decide

Despite several bills on assisted dying being put forward over the years Parliament has failed to agree. Public opinion is divided and politicians do not want to pass controversial laws that may lose votes. It is also hard to ensure a balance between protecting the vulnerable and allowing personal autonomy.

Protecting the vulnerable was a factor in the following case. In **Conway v SS for Justice 2017**, a man who had less than six months to live wanted to choose the time of his death. He argued that the blanket ban on assisted suicide was contrary to **A 8**. The court found that it was *"appropriate to identify protection of the sanctity of life as a moral view regarding the importance of human life as one of the aims promoted by **s 2**"* and thought the law achieved a fair balance between the interests of the wider community and the interests of people in his position. One point in favour of the ban was that if it were relaxed patients (particularly vulnerable and elderly patients) would have less confidence in their doctors and the advice they might give. So it is not only protection from potential beneficiaries or family members, the court clearly thought people needed the protection **s 2** gives as reassurance that doctors would not make a decision lightly because if they did they could face prosecution.

Cases on withdrawal of treatment have also ended up in the European Court of Human Rights (ECtHR). If doctors wish to withdraw treatment against the wishes of the parents it is right that the law should be involved. In **Gosh v Gard 2017** the SC made a similar decision to that in **Bland** in respect of withdrawal of life support for a terminally ill baby. However the parents took the case to the ECtHR because they wanted to take the baby to America for experimental therapy (against the advice of the doctors). The court eventually ruled in favour of the doctors because the baby was suffering and there was no hope of success. Cases like this need to go to court. It was important for the law to get involved because the doctors and the family did not agree on what was best for the child. Where the family and doctors agree it may be unreasonable to use time and money on going to court in a situation where the law has been made clear.

Although not in the specifications you may see reference to **A 9** rights in cases because these are often claimed alongside the right to a private and family life under **A 8**. The question of whether the law should be involved in what is essentially a moral issue arises in most **A 9** cases, as these involve the right to freedom of thought, conscience and religion. In **S.A.S v France 2014** the ECtHR held that France had not violated rights under **A 8** and **A 9** by banning full face veils. The law was not arbitrary (an important issue in human rights law) because it applied to everyone equally and was aimed at encouraging people to live together in harmony.

In **Eweida and others v British Airways 2010**, a Christian employee was suspended from work for openly wearing a cross on a neck chain, in contravention of the company's dress code. She failed in her attempt to prove she had been discriminated against in the tribunals and courts of the UK. However, when the case went to the ECtHR she succeeded on the basis that the policy breached her **A 9** rights.

As with most human rights law, if there is a good reason for the policy, it applies to everyone (**S.A.S v France**) and it is proportionate, the decision may be different. Ms Chaplin was one of the other people bringing an action in the **Eweida** case. She was a nurse who had been told not to wear a cross at work because patients could grab it. She lost because the aim of the policy was for health and safety reasons. The rule applied to everyone and it was proportionate to this aim.

Task 8

Choose two civil cases and make some notes on the moral issues involved. Then add your view of whether the matter should have been a question of law or left to individual choice.

2.10 Changing moral values and changing technology

Sometimes the law changes to reflect changing social values, as we saw with **R v R** where society's views had changed and the law changed to reflect this. Similarly, with the legalisation of prostitution following the **Wolfenden Committee** report. Many anti-discrimination and equality laws have evolved over a long period of time giving increasing rights to women, blacks, ethnic minorities and others. An example of how the law may evolve over time to reflect the changing moral landscape is gay marriage.

Example

The laws on homosexuality have changed as society has changed its views. The development shows the influence of morality upon the law. It is also an example of the length of time it can take for things to change. In 1895, the playwright Oscar Wilde was imprisoned for homosexual behaviour. The **Sexual Offences Act 1967** finally made homosexual acts in private legal (again following the Wolfenden Committee report). The **Civil Partnership Act 2004** regulated gay partnerships and allowed people of the same sex to enjoy many of the rights that married heterosexual couples have. In 2014, gay marriage itself became legal when **s 1** of the **Marriage (Same Sex Couples) Act 2013** came into force, equalising the rights of heterosexuals and gays. Elton John and his partner David Furnish were among the first to marry in 2014.

The law may have to intervene to deal with medical advances, especially where attitudes to these are in conflict, as in **Quintavalle**. However, some changes in technology may be left outside the law, to be dealt with as moral problems. New technology has led to the ability to download films and music via apps. This has led to questions regarding the morality of doing this where it means the producers will lose money. When appointing a new director of Creative Future in 2014, Hollywood said its strategy was to try for voluntary agreements, rather than legislation, on streaming films. The director said it would be better if children were taught that it was wrong and so would avoid doing it due to social pressure rather than because it is illegal. As I pointed out at the beginning of the chapter, this is the way the breaking of moral rules is dealt with.

Advances in technology have led to increased problems with privacy and issues such as the hacking of mobile phones and the retention of data contained in mobile phones and emails. Problems have arisen in social media with online bullying, and cyber-crime in general is becoming an issue. In these cases it is important to have laws in place to regulate behaviour. Mill would agree because harm is caused to others. CCTV has been around a long time but it was the fact that the footage was seen by so many people through social media that led to the conviction of the couple who had sex in the pizza parlour. Privacy is a growing problem because access to information is increasingly easier to obtain. Since Edward Snowden highlighted the fact that governments indiscriminately collect huge amounts of personal data about their citizens in 2013, there have been countless challenges to laws allowing this. These have led to cases in the UK courts, the Court of Justice of the European Union (CJEU) and the European Court of Human Rights.

Examples

In **Home Secretary v Tom Watson & Others 2016**, UK law which requires service providers to retain information contained in emails was found to contravene EU law. The EU law contained in the **Data Protection Directive 1995** offers greater protection against the retention of personal data. The CJEU ruled that under EU law governments are prohibited from the general and indiscriminate retention of data unless it is strictly necessary for the fighting of serious crime. There must also be a connection between the retention of the data and the end objective. The **e-Privacy Directive 2002** built on the above law and extended the protection to the retention of electronic communications In **Andrew v MPC 2017**, the CA held that a police inspector and her husband should receive compensation based on the illegal obtaining and retention of their mobile phone data.

There is currently (December 2017) a case in the ECtHR brought by Amnesty International and other human rights organisations. This is to challenge the law on gathering data. The **Investigatory Powers Act 2016** is the UK's most recent effort and Amnesty say that although the challenge is to the earlier law (the case began in a UK tribunal in 2013) the 2016 law is even more intrusive. They brought the case *"to call an end to the UK government's mass surveillance and unregulated data sharing"*.

You can see that these are difficult issues. Many of the above examples reflect the problem with the law enforcing morality where opinions differ, where there is no 'shared morality'. There are also difficulties where there is a conflict between moral principles such as privacy and other personal freedoms and the public interest, e.g., in security. Snowden thought the gathering of personal information was morally wrong and he broke the law in order to bring the issue to the attention of the public. Moral principles have led to other cases of law-breaking which you may have seen when studying jury equity, e.g., criminal damage by environmental campaigners and the Ponting case on the **Official Secrets Act**. Such acts might follow natural law but go against the positivist view.

There are many other examples of moral issues that have been argued as needing regulation by law. These include smacking children, drinking in the street, swearing, cheating, sunbathing in the nude etc. Look in the newspapers or watch the news and see what interests you. Then think about whether it should be against the law or not. One 2012 example from Russia concerned the punk group Pussy Riot. The group of female singers was convicted of blasphemy and imprisoned after singing protest songs in a cathedral. There was world-wide condemnation of the legal decision, including most Russians who believed the court overreacted. Those who believe in individual freedoms such as Mill would agree. It may, arguably, have been immoral but no-one was harmed. One could argue that it should not have resulted in legal sanctions at all, let alone imprisonment.

Evaluation pointer

Some councils ban drinking on the street and other public places, some don't. It is arguable that this is a matter of morality rather than law. Also, both justice and the rule of law require that the law should apply equally to everyone. It does not seem fair that what is legal in one area is illegal in another.

Here is a final case highlighting the relationship between law and morals and the difficulties posed by advanced technology. It is also an example of the principle that if children are 'Gillick competent', they should be able to make decisions for themselves.

In **JS 2016**, a girl of fourteen who was dying of cancer applied to the court for an order that would allow her body to be cryonically preserved after her death. The judge noted that this was *"an example of the new questions that science poses to the law"*. The case went to court because a child under eighteen cannot make a will to ensure any such requests are complied with at the time of death, and her separated parents were in conflict about it. Also, the body would have to be prepared in a special way before being transported to the United States where the procedure would take place and the **Human Tissue Act 2004** did not cover the situation. The case illustrates how new technology can pose new moral problems.

Recognising it was a difficult task, the judge repeated an oft quoted phrase, that *"hard cases make bad law"*. In separating law and morals he made clear that the case was not about whether cryonic preservation was morally right or wrong, but that the application had to be decided *"in accordance with established principle*". It was not for the court to decide on the arrangements but to resolve the dispute about them. As the mother supported the girl the answer was to make orders placing responsibility in her hands and to prevent the father from intervening. This is an example of the separation of law and morals. The judge did not make an order allowing the procedure; he made an order making the mother solely responsible and prohibiting the father from interfering. This had the result that the procedure went ahead, but at the behest of the mother not the court. (Just as a point of interest, following the decision, the judge in this case visited the girl in the hospice at her request. He found her to be intelligent and competent and clear about what she wanted.)

Task 9

Look at the following examples of the law being involved in moral issues. Give one argument in favour of the law regulating such behaviour and one against

Smacking

Under the **Children Act 2004**, smacking is no longer lawful if it causes bruising or cuts, but is otherwise legal.

Praying

Daily collective worship is a legal requirement in schools under **S 70 of the School Standards and Framework Act 1998** – should the law be involved in what is essentially a purely moral issue?

Force feeding

In **Re E 2012**, a High Court judge ruled that a person suffering from anorexia could be force-fed against her wishes, as it was in her own best interests. The court said the balance should tip in favour of giving life-preserving treatment.

Withdrawing food

In **Re M 2011**, the High Court ruled that withdrawing artificial feeding from a patient in a coma was not in their best interests despite the family wanting the doctors to do this, as in **Bland 1993**.

Summary 1: The differences

1. Both law and morals are based on rules which govern behaviour, but there are differences

moral rules

- develop through opinions over time and don't change overnight
- ought to be obeyed
- are enforced by peer pressure and self-guilt
- are voluntary and apply to those who agree to be bound by them

legal rules

- can change instantly by Act of Parliament or precedent
- must be obeyed
- are enforced by the courts imposing sanctions
- are not voluntary and apply to everyone

Summary 2: The views

2. Views on the relationship between law and morals

Patrick Devlin

- law and morals are related

HLA Hart

- law and morals are separate

John Stuart Mill

- the law should only interfere in moral matters where people need protection from harm

Summary 3: The similarities

3. The similarities between law and morals

crime

- many crimes are both illegal and immoral, e.g., murder and rape

contract

- contracts are based on an exchange of promises and the law will act if these promises are broken, e.g., breach of contract leads to compensation being paid

tort

- the law of tort can be used to protect people from harm by another's negligence, e.g., 'do not harm your neighbour' – **Donoghue**

Examination tip

Read the question carefully for specifics. Use cases and Acts to show the relationship between law and morals – or, if you prefer, to show there isn't one. There is no right answer and much debate as regards this relationship, so form your own opinion. However, a word of warning: avoid voicing personal views too strongly, and ALWAYS support what you say with examples and academic discussion.

Self-test questions

1. *Summarise the opposing views held by the Law Lords in* ***Brown****.*
2. *What is the basic distinction between Hart and Devlin's views?*
3. *What was the outcome of* ***Quintavalle****?*
4. *What is the* ***Wolfenden Report*** *about?*
5. *Make a list of 3 differences between law and morals.*

For answers to the tasks and self-test questions, please go to my website at www.drsr.org and click the button 'Answers to Kindle tasks'

"Everyone seems to have a view of the proper outcome. I am very well aware of the inevitability that our answer will be applauded by some but that as many will be offended by it"

Ward LJ

By the end of this Chapter you should be able to:

- ***Explain some of the different theories about what is meant by the term 'justice'***
- ***Evaluate the role of both formal and substantive justice in the legal system***
- ***Illustrate your evaluation by reference to cases and examples***

3.1 The meaning of justice

Many people see law and justice as the same thing but this not necessarily the case. It is quite possible to have unjust laws. It is also possible to have unjust outcomes from just laws. That said, in liberal democracies at least, it is the primary aim of any legal system to deliver justice. Unjust laws are likely to be challenged and may become unenforceable. An example is the poll tax in the 80s. It was widely thought that the tax was unfair and enough people, from many different social groups, demonstrated against it to force a change in the law.

So what is justice? A simple notion of justice is that of fairness or equality – treating everyone equally. When you hear someone say "But that's not fair!" it usually means, "You aren't treating everyone the same." Protests against discrimination of various kinds have led to changes over the years as we saw in the last chapter. There are now laws against many types of discrimination and these have evolved over time. However, justice can mean different things to different people. There are several theories on the subject. You should be able to discuss some of them.

Examination tip

Don't try to learn all of the theories outlined here. You won't have time to discuss many of them, so use ones that make sense to you. Your essay will be more confident and it will be easier for you to use examples. A few theorists well explained and illustrated with examples will earn more marks than a recitation of several without developing any of them. It is sensible to be able to explain natural law, positivism and utilitarianism because you can use those theories in an essay on law and morals too. Learn at least one theorist from each of those and add an economic theory and you will have a sound base.

Many books have been written by, and about, the people putting forward different theories. It is a good idea to try to read someone first-hand if possible. You will get a much better feel for what they mean than you will by merely reading what I say about them. However, you do not need the depth of knowledge that would be contained in books on specific theories of justice. As with the diversity of moral views, there is a huge diversity of opinion on what justice means and how (and whether) the law can achieve it. Whether justice is achieved depends on your view of justice. If you believe justice should mean equality then a law that does not provide for equality will not, in your opinion, achieve justice. Many see justice as the fair distribution of benefits and burdens in society, but you will see that opinions differ on the form that distribution should take. As much is a matter of opinion you should try to look at the law (an Act of Parliament, a case or the legal process) from the viewpoint of one or more of the theorists. This will give you a wider view and you will be able to compare your opinion of whether justice is achieved with another theory. What follows is an outline of the main theories. This is followed by a discussion of how far the law achieves justice and then by examples from across the specifications.

3.2 The theories of justice

As noted above there are different views on how law and justice should be defined. Justice may be based on equality, fairness, a distribution of wealth and resources or an achievement of the greatest benefit. This means you cannot pigeonhole a law and say it belongs to one particular theory. You can however, use a theory to help to analyse a law. You had a brief introduction to the theories earlier; here they are in a bit more detail.

Examination tip

There is no 'right' theory and you will see they are sometimes in direct conflict. Don't try to choose a theory that you think the examiner will agree with; you can't. What you need to be able to do is explain a law or case in terms of one or more of the theories. You could choose a case and then say how a positivist would see it and whether a positivist would believe it achieved justice. You can also say what your opinion is, as long as you can back it up and use a theory to compare it to. You could refer to your chosen case and say, e.g., that you don't think it achieved justice because the decision did not reflect morality. It therefore went against natural law even though it achieved justice according to a positivist. The ability to be able to identify that a law would be seen as just under one theory and unjust under another is a skill that will be rewarded by the examiner.

Natural law

The natural law theory regards law as coming from a higher source. Laws are based on moral rules. The origins of natural Law theories lie with **Aristotle** and **St Thomas Aquinas**.

Aristotle (384 – 322 BCE) said that moral rules come from nature. We have 'natural' rights. He argued that the basis of justice is fairness, and that this takes two forms:

Distributive justice – the law acts to distribute benefits and burdens fairly throughout society. This can occur through various laws governing property rights, e.g., in the law of theft and contract.

Corrective justice – the law acts to correct attempts by individuals to disturb this fair distribution. In criminal law, confiscation, compensation and restitution are corrective sentences. In civil law, D pays compensation to correct any wrongdoing. Corrective law is seen in any cases or procedures where the law has tried to correct an imbalance.

Example

Football is played by equal numbers on both sides, using the same pitch, the same ball and the same-sized goals. If one team's goal were smaller than the other team's, that would be a breach of *distributive justice* – it wouldn't be treating the teams fairly. When a player breaks the rules, the referee (another word for 'judge', of course) may award a penalty, a free kick, send the offending player off the pitch or whatever. In this case, the referee is using *corrective justice* – trying to compensate one team for the offence of the other.

Saint Thomas Aquinas (1227 – 1274) said that moral rules come from God and that people should do good and avoid evil. We have 'God-given' rights. He suggested that any law which went against morality would not be just. If a law is not a just law, we need not obey it. This is because it is not a 'true' law. However, he also said that such a law should be obeyed if *not* obeying it would disrupt society. This is because that would not be in accordance with God's will either. Like Aristotle, Aquinas also looked at how the benefits and burdens in society should be distributed and how any disturbance of the distribution should be corrected.

Distributive justice is also part of the economic theories of justice so there is more on this later.

Many countries have a constitution which sets out certain rights. These are seen as a higher form of law. If a law were passed which conflicted with constitutional rights, it could be subject to challenge. Britain does not have a written constitution. However, the **Human Rights Act 1998** has provided that the 'natural' rights set out in the **European Convention on Human Rights** are now part of UK law. If you are studying human rights it is a useful topic to illustrate many of the concepts of law.

Example

The right to life is a 'natural' right so murder, assisted suicide and euthanasia are both immoral and against the natural law view of justice. This distinction may be important in euthanasia cases because technology allows people to be kept alive artificially for so long nowadays. The law may have to step in to decide whose rights should be protected. The sanctity of life must be balanced against personal autonomy – the right of people to choose the time of their own death, as in assisted suicide cases. Supporters of natural law would say the law will achieve justice by protecting the right to life.

Positivism

Positivists have tried to find a more scientific way of describing law, without reference to morality. For positivists, law *may* be based on ideas of morality or justice, but these are not *necessary*. The validity of law is not affected by whether it is morally acceptable. Most positivist theories attempt to explain what law *is* rather than what it *ought* to be. Although this means that a law is valid even if it is unjust or immoral, it does not mean it has to be followed blindly. Most positivists acknowledge that there may be times when a law should not be obeyed. What they *do* say is that even though it is unjust, it is still *law*.

Two important positivists are **Kelsen** and **Hart**.

Kelsen (1881 – 1973) felt it was impossible to define justice. He tried to provide a science of law which excluded any political or moral content. He based his theory on a set of 'legal norms'. He saw law as a form of social control. The legal norm imposes duties or confers powers on officials to apply sanctions; an example is giving judges the power to impose sentences and provide remedies.

Hart (1907 – 1992) distinguished between 'procedural justice' and 'substantive justice'.

The first he called 'justice *according* to law' and this involves questions of whether the *legal process* is just. Examples would be having access to justice, the right to appeal and jury trials.

The second he called 'justice *of* the law' and this looks at whether the *law itself* is just. For example to be just a law would have to apply to everyone equally. If it didn't the law should try to correct any imbalance as it does with consumer protection laws.

To Hart, the law is based purely on rules and is separate from issues of morality. This seems to mean the state should not use the law to enforce morality. However, Hart accepted that it could use the law to stop people causing harm, whether to others or themselves. His paternalistic view of law extended to using the law to prevent a threat to the dominant view in society. This seems quite close to the natural law view that the law should protect the public from immorality. However, as we saw in the previous chapter, Hart would not accept something should be illegal if it did not hurt society, so supported the Wolfenden Committee. He might have been against assisted suicide as he would want people to be protected against harming themselves, but he supported liberalising the laws on homosexuality and prostitution.

Despite Hart's ambivalence, positivism is opposed to natural law theories. For a positivist, a bad law would still be valid and have to be obeyed. A natural law theorist would disagree. Nazi law is often used as an example. Positivists might say laws discriminating against Jewish people should be obeyed. Natural law theorists would argue that law must follow some 'higher natural law' and if it did not it would not be 'true' law. The segregation of African Americans in the USA, and the apartheid laws of South Africa, are other examples.

Evaluation pointer

Parliamentary supremacy in the English legal system means that Parliament can make any law it likes. If Parliament passes an immoral law, no judge can say it isn't just and people don't have to obey it. This is not much of a problem in a democracy, as unfair laws will lead to protests, as with the poll tax in the 1980s. So many different groups were against what was seen as an unfair tax that the government had to put another law before Parliament to change it. The law was valid even though unjust, but the protests led to change to a fairer system. In less democratic societies, it is more of a problem, as seen above.

Utilitarianism

Utilitarianism looks at the *consequences* of a law, and asks whether it benefits more people than it harms. If a law 'maximises happiness', i.e., increases the total happiness or welfare of a society, it is just. Utilitarianism is often simplified as 'the greatest good for the greatest number'. However, utility is not concerned with *equal* distribution of happiness, but with *total* happiness. It can therefore lead to injustice because if there are a few extremely happy people, then total happiness may be greater even if there are lots of slightly unhappy people. Utilitarianism focuses on the needs of society rather than the individual. It is in conflict with individual rights and freedoms and is criticised by libertarians, who see the rights of the individual as all-important.

Jeremy Bentham (1748-1832) was a utilitarian. He had little time for individual rights in the sense of natural rights, which he referred to as "*nonsense on stilts*". His utilitarian theory was an attack on the natural law theory. He tried to produce a more scientific approach to justice. He suggested that law should be evaluated by reference to the principle of utility, and not by reference to a "*misguided belief*" in natural law and natural rights.

Example

A law is passed which bans smoking in public. A utilitarian would argue that the rights of the majority to protection from health risks outweigh the rights of the individual to smoke because the 'greatest number' benefit from the ban. This law would therefore be just. Some years ago, when more people smoked, a utilitarian might argue against such a law.

The problem with utilitarianism is that it ignores individual rights, unless increasing those rights benefits society. The introduction of the **Human Rights Act 1998** and the **ECHR** that it enshrined increases the rights of individuals. This appears to be against the utilitarian theory, but it can be argued that society itself benefits from certain rights being enshrined in law and so increases the greater good.

Similarly, anti-terrorism laws are arguably for the greater good of society. At one time, suspects could be held indefinitely without being charged. A utilitarian could argue that the ends justify the means. An alternative argument would be that society itself is weakened by going against the rule of law. These laws could be seen as against 'natural' law as they conflict with the rule that no-one should be imprisoned without a fair trial. This is also against the rule of law.

The **Terrorism Act 2006** removed the indefinite detention of suspects without charge and changed it to 28 days. This was increased to 42 days by the **Counter-Terrorism Act 2008**. The **Protection of Freedoms Act 2012** has reduced it to 14 days. This shows the difficulties of achieving justice for everyone. We all want to be safe, but few people want to live in a society that can lock people up without any charges being brought against them. In **A v the Home Department 2005**, Lord Hoffman said of the law under the **2001 Act** that the real threat to the nation came not from terrorism *"but from laws such as these"*.

John Stuart Mill (1806-1883) was a leading utilitarian and is still influential today. As we saw in the previous chapter, Mill was also a libertarian and attempted to unite the ideas of utilitarianism and individual rights. He had a minimalist approach to law, arguing that people should have the right to act unless exercising that right harmed others. Only then should the law interfere to restrict those rights.

Task 10

Make a note of whether Mill would have agreed with the following two laws and add what you think Hart would have said about them:

the statute law against drinking and driving

the statute law making the use of seat belts compulsory

Note that utilitarianism and positivism overlap.

- ***Positivism separates legal rules (law) from social rules (morals).***
- ***Utilitarianism focuses on the consequences of the rules.***

Economic and social theories

Many economic theories are modern alternatives to utilitarianism. Traditionally, utilitarianism looks at maximising happiness. Economic theories try to measure this in terms of wealth and look at how, and whether, the state should use the law to re-distribute wealth to achieve a just society, e.g., by way of taxation. Three important economic theorists are Karl **Marx**, John **Rawls** and Robert **Nozick**.

Marx (1818 – 1883) believed that the law only served the ruling classes, those who *"own the means of production"*. He wanted to see distributive justice (remember Aristotle?): *"from each according to his ability, to each according to his needs"* and thought the state should intervene to redistribute wealth. Marx did not support *equal* distribution, but distribution according to ability and need. He did not address individual rights as he saw these as reducing the power of people to work together for change.

Rawls (1921 – 2002) argued that utilitarianism was flawed because it failed to take account of the *"separateness of persons"*. His theory is based on what rules a group of individuals would choose in order to make their society just – what earlier writers had called a 'social contract'. This type of justice involves re-distributing benefits and burdens within society. Rawls added a new feature to the group called the *"veil of ignorance"*. This means that the individuals making the rules would not know who they were and so could not be influenced by self-interest. Think back to your desert island in Task 2. In Rawls' view, your rules should be made in ignorance of your wealth or status and any personal characteristics. If people do not know whether they are rich or poor, young or old, male or female, Jews or Christians, able or disabled etc., then they will agree only to rules which would protect them *whatever* their circumstances. Such rules would therefore achieve justice. This theory of justice is egalitarian, based on equality. It also emphasises individual rights as the rules are based on what is best for everyone as individuals, whether rich or poor etc. There will be fundamental rights that will not be sacrificed to the common good.

Nozick (1938 – 2002) argued that for a just society there should be minimal interference in people's lives by law and state. Although he too rejected the utilitarian argument, he did not agree with **Rawls** that benefits and burdens should be redistributed. He argued that if people come by something fairly, then the law should not attempt any redistribution because that would interfere with people's rights to their property. *How* goods or wealth were distributed within society would be just, as long as everyone *received* their property in a just manner.

Example and Evaluation pointer

In **Rogers v Swindon NHS Primary Care Trust 2006**, a woman took her local Health Trust to court for not supplying a new drug, Herceptin, shown to reduce the risk of recurrence of breast cancer. It cost £20,000 per year and was not yet available on the NHS. The CA held that the refusal to consider her for treatment was illegal because it was based on personal circumstances rather than clinical needs. The law is not telling the hospital trust to give or withhold the drugs; it is requiring the trust to consider the particular circumstances and follow the correct procedures when making a decision. Thus, in a similar case in 2008, a challenge to the decision of many Primary Care Trusts not to fund the use of the drug Lucentis, which has been shown to improve the vision of people suffering from certain eye disorders which could lead to blindness, failed. In 2017, a hospital trust had refused to supply a new drug, Kuvan, to a child who was unable to undergo the usual treatment. The court held that these were special circumstances which the trust should have taken into account. Later that year the trust reconsidered the case and provided the treatment. These decisions raise several questions which could be considered when evaluating justice.

Should all Hospital Trusts be made to supply life-saving drugs?

Should the Trust make the decision on a case-by-case basis, depending on available funds?

Should the money be used to treat several other patients with more minor problems?

Hospitals and doctors with limited resources face these difficult economic issues every day. Sometimes the law has to get involved to resolve the conflict (by balancing the competing interests).

The CA's point in **Rogers** was not that all treatment should be funded, but that the policy in relation to funding should be fairer and more transparent. A fairer policy would be a type of distributive justice. However, funding one person at too high a cost to the public and at the price of denying treatment to many other people in need would not fit the utilitarian assessment of justice.

Critics of utilitarianism, such as Rawls argue that it is impossible to define what is 'good' in order to calculate the greatest good for the greatest number. It is a fair point: what is good for one person may not be for another. This can be seen in the conflicting views on fox-hunting (the **Hunting Act**) and sado-masochism (**Brown**) and raises the issue of whether the law should intervene to prevent such practices. One type of utilitarianism looks at preferences rather than the greatest good. Justice is achieved where most preferences are satisfied. However, this also has problems where all preferences are included, even objectionable ones, e.g., if a society is racist or patriarchal then ethnic minorities and women will be subordinated. Nazi laws discriminating against Jewish people in Germany, segregation laws in America and apartheid laws in South Africa are examples we have already noted. Positivists might say such laws should be obeyed as long as properly made. Natural law theorists might say such laws are immoral so need not be followed.

The type of society will influence the preferences and therefore the law. In **Brown**, the perceived preferences of society were that the acts were immoral and should be illegal. This outweighed the preferences of the participants. A problem with any type of utilitarianism is that it can result in serious injustice. It would accept torture as a means of getting information to find a bomb before it is set to go off. It would accept killing a person blocking an emergency exit when people are trying to abandon a sinking ship (this happened in a ferry disaster in 1987). The justification is that the wrong is done to one person to save others. The latter approach can be seen in **Re A**, where one twin died (and some would say was killed) in order to save the other. That was arguably justified as she would have died in any case. It is more difficult where the person killed would not otherwise have died. A form of distributive justice which does not focus on total happiness would seem more acceptable. Hart, for example, would view a fair distribution as more important than total happiness.

Another theorist, the academic Ronald **Dworkin**, believed that certain rights should not be denied to individuals even if to do so would benefit society. He believed, like Mill, in personal autonomy but wrote that there was no general right to liberty, only to specific liberties. Some specific rights would be inalienable and the state would not be able to override these rights. Other rights could be subject to state intervention if it advanced the overall welfare of society. An example is **Home Secretary v Tom Watson & Others 2016** where the Court of Justice of the European Union ruled that governments were prohibited by the **Data Protection Directive 1995** and the **e-Privacy Directive 2002**, from the general and indiscriminate retention of data unless it was strictly necessary for the fighting of serious crime. So, a state is not totally prohibited from retaining or using data because the right to privacy can be overridden if it is for the welfare of society, i.e., for security or the prevention of serious crime. Rights under the **ECHR** are inalienable but the state can derogate from most of these provisions in the interests of public health or security (have a look at how the 2017 Amnesty case developed). This distributes the benefits and burdens more fairly than the utilitarian method. Individual rights are protected but the interests of society as a whole are also taken into account. A bit more on how distributive justice works in practice and according to the theorists may help to explain.

3.3 Distributive justice in practice

Durkheim (see Chapter 2) saw the law as a means of ensuring that social structures worked. Distributive justice is based on the social theory of sharing burdens (the payment of taxes and the carrying out of duties in society) and benefits (the receipt of money, property and other resources) fairly within a community. The state will use the law as a way of social engineering, to manipulate access to benefits (health, education and other resources) and to regulate burdens (taxes, duties and obligations to behave in a certain way).

Example

The **Rogers** case provides an example of how distributive justice would apply in practice.

A utilitarian would want the hospital resources distributed to provide the greatest benefit for the most people. This could mean not giving expensive drugs to one patient, but instead using the funds to give more people a chance of a cure, or a better quality of life as long as this achieved the maximum happiness overall. Marx would want any such distribution to depend on the needs of the patient. Rawls would probably prefer an egalitarian approach, so that resources were shared more equally. The problem with achieving justice under any one theory is that resources are limited so not everyone will be satisfied.

The National Institute for Clinical Excellence (NICE) published a report in August 2008. This adopted the utilitarian approach and said that if drugs are too expensive the NHS should not have to provide them, even if they would prolong life. This approach means Health Care Trusts have a stronger argument against prescribing expensive drugs. If treatment is expensive and funds have to be allocated from limited resources, this will reduce what is available for other patients.

Some countries have discrimination laws which will mean that differences in, e.g., sex, colour or religion would not affect the distribution of any benefits or burdens; everyone would be treated the same. Other countries do not have such laws, which will mean the distribution can be unbalanced. This was the case in many countries in the EU before workers were given the right to equal pay for equal work regardless of sex. Equal treatment laws were later extended to prohibit other types of discrimination, but these laws apply only to members of the EU or to other countries which have chosen to implement them. So how the burdens and benefits are shared differs according to national policies. It also differs according to the different theories.

Example

The **Jobseekers Allowance (Employment, Skills and Enterprise Scheme) Regulations 2011** provided that jobseekers had to take unpaid work to avoid their benefits being reduced. This included work that was nothing to do with their skills or career plans and was challenged in court by way of judicial review. The CA ruled the Regulations were illegal because the correct procedure had not been followed by the government minister. Instead of remaking the law to comply with the correct procedure the government rushed a bill through Parliament which overturned the court's decision. This is the **Jobseekers (Back to Work Schemes) Act 2013**. The scheme is now covered by primary legislation enacted by Parliament so cannot be challenged in court. Some argue that the provision of unemployment benefits is wrong in itself and the law should not provide for it because it rewards people who won't work as well as those who can't. What would the theorists think?

Marx's distribution was based on ability and need. He was not overly concerned with law, but social policy, and the receipt of a benefit was not necessarily balanced against a burden. People contributed to society what they were able to and those who did not contribute could still receive benefits according to need. His type of distributive theory could support the jobseekers as they would not have to contribute to receive a benefit. However, they would be expected to give according to their ability. This would probably extend to trying to find work, but might not to being forced to take unpaid work.

Aristotle's distribution was based on worth and would support the government's view unless the jobseekers could show they had contributed (arguably by waiting for a more suitable job which might pay more, so they would pay more in taxes). This type of distribution would not necessarily help prevent social injustice. People would only get benefits from society according to what they contributed to society, which is similar to the first part of Marxist distribution but stops there. It does not extend benefits to those in need (unless they have contributed). Aristotle would consider distribution according to need as unjust because it would benefit people who were lazy and made no contribution. His theory can lead to social injustice, especially if extended to the elderly and infirm and others who cannot, rather than will not, contribute. Some say that this injustice can be avoided by looking at earlier contributions (work done, taxes paid and any other contribution to the community). However, it is not always the case and could exclude people severely disabled from a young age.

Aquinas' distribution is similar to that of Aristotle but with distribution not only depending on worth. He proposed allocating benefits based on merit and need and also according to a person's standing in society. This could include those in need getting social housing, free education, free health care and other benefits such as the jobseekers allowance. However, it would also mean that the ruling classes were entitled to more of society's benefits than those of lower status, and a jobseeker is quite likely to be low in the ranking.

Rawls would support an equal distribution of benefits and burdens. If someone has paid taxes and/or made social security contributions then they should be entitled to a share of the benefits, e.g., the jobseekers allowance.

Task 11

What should go in the right-hand column in the table below?

What is the theory?

We believe that law is separate from morality. We base our understanding of the law on rules to be obeyed – what some call legal norms. A law may be unjust but it is still a law.	Our theory is described as
We are concerned to maximise happiness. Some of us reject individual rights but others believe that the law should only interfere if someone exercising a right harms others.	Our theory is described as
We believe law is closely linked to morality and that moral rules come from a higher authority than the law. Unjust law is not true law.	Our theory is described as

3.4 How far does the law achieve justice?

Several examples have already been given but what follows provides a more detailed analysis of how and whether the law achieves justice. There are plenty more examples to be found and you can refer to all areas of the law you have studied for other ideas on the extent to which substantive legal rules, institutions and processes achieve justice. When you study a topic, ask yourself the following questions.

- ***Is the legal system just (procedural justice)?***
- ***Is a particular law just (substantive justice)?***

It is important to realise that the distinctions between the different words used to describe justice (substantive, procedural, corrective, distributive etc.) are merely ways of trying to explain and analyse the concept. No one description is correct or exclusive. Substantive justice is concerned with whether the law itself is just. Formal justice is concerned with whether the process is just. Both may – or may not – include distributive justice and corrective justice.

Example

The **Consumer Rights Act** provides substantive contract law rights. It corrects the inequality between a manufacturer and consumer and a retailer and consumer and ensures a fairer distribution of benefits and burdens. **PACE** provides procedural law rights. It corrects the imbalance between the law enforcement agencies and suspects by distributing the benefits and burdens more fairly (giving rights to suspects and imposing a corresponding duty on the police).

The different ways of describing justice may also be in conflict. It is possible to have substantive justice but not satisfy the requirements of formal justice because the system is flawed in some way. It is also possible for the process to work well but the law itself to be unfair.

Here are a few more ideas to help you explain and illustrate the ways to describe justice.

Procedural justice – legal institutions and process

Procedural justice is also known as formal justice because it looks at the form rather than the substance of the law. Justice requires that there is a system of independent tribunals for the administration of law and the resolution of disputes (what Hart called 'justice *according* to law'). Procedural justice would also include trial by jury, appointment and independence of judges, financing of court cases, sentencing, remedies and so on.

Example

There was much public concern in January 2018 when it was reported that Jon Venables, one of the two killers of the toddler Jamie Bulger in 1993, was to be tried in secret after re-offending. He was returned to prison and then charged for possessing indecent images of children. After his conviction for murder he had been granted anonymity because of serious threats to kill him and in an attempt at rehabilitation. He was only aged ten at the time and served eight years. However, he has reoffended twice since his release and many do not feel justice is served by continuing his anonymity. It is part of the rule of law that justice must not only be done but be seen to be done. Arguably, anonymity could be achieved by using a screen or video link rather than having the whole trial in secret. The pressure group Justice, said: "The principle of open justice is integral to the operation of our courts and the right to a fair trial. It ensures that justice is seen to be done, safeguards against arbitrary decision making and maintains public confidence in the justice system.

When evaluating procedural justice you could discuss:

The **appeals system** aims at ensuring justice by allowing appeals to a higher court. Once the appeals system has been exhausted there is still a way of achieving justice. This is aimed at correcting any initial injustice.

The **Criminal Cases Review Commission** (CCRC) was set up in 1995 with the sole purpose of correcting injustice. Its establishment is a clear acknowledgement by the state that injustices do occur. It is a vital safety net for those for whom the appeals system has failed to achieve justice. There are many famous cases such as the Guildford four and the Birmingham six, where the CCRC succeeded in having the convictions overturned after fifteen and sixteen years in jail respectively. **Kennedy 2007** is an example you should know from your study of manslaughter. Another is **Evans 2016** where a footballer who had served two and a half years for rape had his conviction overturned after a referral by the CCRC and a retrial. A referral for appeal has to be based on new evidence or a point of law not previously considered. The **Criminal Cases Review Commission (Information) Act 2016** amends the **Criminal Appeal Act 1995** and extends the powers of the CCRC to obtain material upon which to base a referral. When looking for new evidence or law, the CCRC can obtain material from public bodies such as the police. The **2016 Act** extends this to private companies or individuals, although a court order is needed. This may further ensure that justice is done as it will be easier to investigate the case.

Another way of achieving justice is by way of **judicial review**. This challenges the form of the law (procedural justice) rather than the substance of the law (substantive justice). Examples include **Pretty**, **Purdy** and **Black** in the previous chapter and the jobseekers case above under distributive justice. Judicial review is a way of correcting an injustice in the law by allowing people affected by it to challenge the way the law was made (Aristotle's corrective justice). That is why the cases are all in the style of 'R on the application of'. R is for Regina who represents the state as in criminal cases. The state brings the action on behalf of the applicant (the person affected). It is common to reduce the name to just refer to the applicant and the department or minister being challenged e.g., **Purdy v DPP**. Judicial review also illustrates the overlap between the different descriptions of justice (procedural, substantive, distributive and corrective).

Jury trial provides what is seen as a fairer system of justice. A jury may decide a case based on what seems right, known as jury equity. This means reaching a verdict according to conscience rather than evidence. An example is **Drake 2008**, where the jury found the group Greenpeace not guilty of criminal damage to a power station despite clear evidence to the contrary. The jury protected the right to protest and freedoms under **A 10** and **A 11 ECHR**. Other cases where juries have acquitted include campaigners causing damage to GM crops. Some would argue that such decisions can be justified on the basis that the law should not prosecute people for causing criminal damage when they are making a legitimate protest. However the downside is inconsistency and there have been cases where protesters have been convicted of criminal damage to GM crops on very similar facts. Jury equity is thus a two-edged sword. E.P. Thompson suggested that the jury judged not only the accused but also the law itself and the acquittal of Greenpeace and other campaigners illustrates this. Auld LJ though that the jury going against the law and the evidence was *"a blatant affront to the legal process"*. Both are valid, though incompatible, views. The positive view is that juries are a safeguard against unjust laws. The negative view is that juries can be inconsistent, as seen in the GM crop cases and also several euthanasia cases where the defence of diminished responsibility has been accepted or rejected on very similar facts.

Another issue with jury trials is where a trial is particularly complex or lengthy. The **Protection of Freedoms Act 2012** repeals the provisions of the **Criminal Justice Act 2003**, which allowed for complex fraud trials to be heard without a jury. In 2017, some jury members said they had suffered stress and had trouble getting back to normal after being on a jury for 20 months in the longest-ever fraud trial. Trial by jury may achieve justice for the accused but if it is at the cost of causing harm to others this goes against most theories of justice.

The later **Act** does not affect the provision which allows for trial without jury where there are fears of jury tampering. The first trial without jury in a major criminal case took place in January 2010, due to fears that the jury could be 'nobbled'. It has long been argued that justice must not only be done, but be seen to be done, and that a trial by one's peers is a major pillar in the legal justice system. Protestors outside the court held placards reading *"No jury. No justice"*. In 2014 the Lord Chief Justice, Lord Thomas, again raised the suggestion that the right to trial by jury should be removed for minor offences and fraud trials. It seems that public opinion regards justice for the accused as more important.

A case that illustrates the roles of the CCRC, the CA and the jury is **Yam 2017**. D had been convicted of murder and the CCRC referred the case to the CA based on new evidence. The CA confirmed that as well as new evidence there must be a real possibility that the conviction would be considered unsafe and restated the point made in **Pendleton 2002** by Lord Bingham who said:

> *"The Court of Appeal is entrusted with a power of review to guard against the possibility of injustice but it is a power to be exercised with caution, mindful that the Court of Appeal is not privy to the jury's deliberations and must not intrude into territory which properly belongs to the jury."*

On the facts the CA found that the new evidence would not have affected the jury's decision so the conviction was safe and the appeal dismissed.

Precedent is based on treating like cases alike (*stare decisis*) which is fair and ensures consistency. Other rules of precedent can be used to avoid injustice caused by too strict an adherence to the *stare decisis* s rule, e.g.:

- **Crime**: The use of the 1966 Practice Statement in **Gemmell 2003** to overrule **Caldwell 1982**
- **Contract**: **Merritt 1971** distinguishing **Balfour 1919**
- **Tort**: Setting an original precedent in **Donoghue v Stevenson 1932**

In **Edwards v Environment Agency (Cemex UK Cement Co Ltd intervening) 2011**, a question arose about the powers of the Supreme Court. The SC confirmed that it had all the powers previously invested in the House of Lords. This included the power to correct any injustice caused by an earlier decision of the House or the Supreme Court, however it might have arisen. Thus the powers given to the HL under the **1966 Practice Statement** have passed to the SC, so earlier decisions can be overruled in the interests of justice.

Access to justice – access to legal advice and representation has been seriously reduced under the **Legal Aid, Sentencing and Punishment of Offenders Act 2012** (**LASPO**). The bill took a long time to get through Parliament but was finally passed. The arguments against the bill were that any system of justice should be based on equality and that if people felt they could not get access to justice they would not believe in the rule of law. However, the Minister for Justice argued that although legal aid is *"an essential part of the justice system"* the money has to come from taxpayers and resources are limited. The shadow justice minister said that any system of justice should be based on equality. This is a matter of distributive justice and raises the question of whether there is a fair balance of benefits and burdens.

Two cases challenging the lack of access to justice since **LASPO** have led to a greater degree of justice. The first was in 2016 and based on the introduction of a residency test before legal aid would be considered. The High Court ruled it unlawful but the CA allowed the government's appeal. The group which brought the case, the Public Law Project, said the decision went against two fundamental principles – that all equally enjoy the protection of ours laws and all are accountable to our courts. This is similar to how Lord Bingham referred to the rule of law (see Chapter 1). People who are subject to the law should also have the protection of the law. This is a form of distributive justice, balancing the burdens and the benefits fairly. In the second case in 2017, brought by the penal reform group the Howard League, the removal of legal aid from some categories of prisoners was challenged. The challenge went to the Supreme Court and was partially successful. The government has ordered a review of the situation which is due to report in 2018.

In the Bach Report on legal aid and access to justice in 2017 the Bach Commission suggests restoring access to legal aid for many social welfare and some family cases, noting that people should have the right *"to receive reasonable legal assistance without costs they cannot afford"*. The report proposes a **Right to Justice Act** to make existing rights to justice legally enforceable. Writing in the New Law Journal in October 2017 David Burrows said *"justice is what judges do"* and rejected the idea of an Act of Parliament giving a right to justice. He added that the right to justice has existed at least since Magna Carta (1215). He agrees with Bach that the rules need simplifying and the scope of legal aid widened (and that this is rightly a job for politicians) but says:

> *"A 'Right to Justice Act' is a very silly idea indeed. One thing our judges do very well already is justice. The more sinister reason is: that which can be given by politicians can be taken away by them".*

The rule of law can also be discussed in connection with the above points because this requires the law to be clear and accessible. The restrictions on legal aid do not conform to the rule. It may be that there needs to be a new Act but it should be one providing access to legal aid and assistance rather than a right to justice. It should also be clearly written so people can understand what their rights are and whether they qualify for assistance. As Burrows says, a right is no right if you do not know about it. In **R (on the application of Unison) v Lord Chancellor 2017**, the SC ruled in favour of a challenge by the trade union Unison to the imposition of fees on those seeking justice in the employment tribunals. Trade unions had referred to these fees, introduced in 2013, as a *"tax on justice"*. The SC ruled that access to tribunals and courts is an essential feature of a society governed by the rule of law. The fees have since been removed. This case is also another example of corrective justice by way of judicial review.

Remedies and sentencing

Remedies and sentencing are both clear examples of Aristotle's corrective justice.

Civil remedies aim to achieve justice by ensuring D compensates C for any wrongdoing. The remedy of damages may be reduced where C has been contributorily negligent. This makes the award of compensation fairer by balancing the actions of both parties. Remedies are a way of correcting any imbalance in distributive justice made in the civil law, e.g., by awarding compensation for a breach of contract or a negligent act that has disturbed the balance.

In sentencing, the aim is to achieve a just balance between the interests of society (deterrence and retribution) and the defendant (rehabilitation). Mitigating and aggravating factors can influence the judge to do what is just in the circumstances. Sentencing is a way of correcting any imbalance in distributive justice caused by a criminal act, e.g., by restoring stolen property and/or punishing D for the crime committed.

Task 12

Choose a procedure, either from the above examples or pick one of your own. Write a paragraph about whether you think it achieves justice, including a theory or two and whether the theory agrees with your view.

Substantive justice – the legal rules

How far does the law achieve justice in the substantive law? (This is Hart's 'justice *of* the law'.) Here are a few ideas from across the specifications, but with the emphasis on criminal law. There are plenty more examples you will come across in your studies because the concept of justice permeates all laws and procedures.

3.5 Justice and criminal law

There is plenty to discuss here. The rules relating to *mens rea*, especially for murder, are problematic. The attempt to achieve justice in the development of the law on intention has left the law uncertain and arguably unjust. One role of law is to provide justice and to punish those at fault. However, strict liability crimes allow a criminal conviction without proof of *mens rea*. This seems unjust so if the Act is silent the courts will presume *mens rea* is needed, as in **Sweet v Parsley 1970**. In **Gemmell & Richards 2003**, the HL used the **1966 Practice Statement** to overrule their earlier decision on recklessness in order to achieve justice. State of affairs crimes such as **Winzar 1983**, seem even more unjust as a person can be guilty without either *actus reus* or *mens rea*. The thin-skull rule also seems unjust because D may be guilty of a greater crime because of the victim's actions, as in **Blaue 1975**.

The correspondence principle requires that the *mens rea* and *actus reus* of a crime should match. This is not true in the case of murder, unlawful act manslaughter and two of the non-fatal offences. These are cases of constructive liability, where the offence is constructed from the *mens rea* of one crime and the *actus reus* of another. The Law Commission has proposed that all crimes should follow the correspondence principle (**Report No 361 of 2015**) and constructive liability should be abolished. Finding someone guilty of such a serious crime as murder where there was no intent to kill (**Stringer 2008**), and of manslaughter where there is only intent to commit some kind of unlawful act (**JF 2015**) does not achieve justice. In the latter case the *mens rea* was only for the minor offence of criminal damage. Case examples for the non-fatal offences include **Mowatt 1968**, **Roberts 1971** and **Savage 1991**.

In **Gilderdale 2010**, a woman who killed her daughter in an assisted suicide was found not guilty of murder by the jury and given a 12-month conditional discharge. The judge said the decision of the jury showed "*common sense, decency and humanity*". Many agreed with the judge and thought justice was done, but many others thought that justice was not done because she had taken a life (a natural law view). In **Inglis 2010**, in similar circumstances, the mother was sentenced to life because she was found guilty of murder. The contrast in sentencing in these cases shows the difficulty in having a mandatory life sentence. Once murder is established the judge has no discretion, so Mrs Inglis was given life even though it was accepted she acted in what she believed were her son's best interests. Justice demands that there is greater consistency in the law. There are many other cases included with morals in the previous chapter.

The defence of diminished responsibility achieves greater justice because the judge has discretion when sentencing, so can take the circumstances into account, as in **Freaney 2011**. This defence is not just when it comes to the burden of proof though. Unlike other defences the burden is on D to prove diminished responsibility. It was confirmed in **Wilcocks 2016** that the **Coroners and Justice Act** (**CJA**) has not changed the **Homicide Act** on this. Perhaps it should have done and so corrected this injustice. As for loss of control under the **CJA**, it can be said the law is now clearer but still does not achieve justice for women because loss of control is still needed – despite a recommendation by the Law Commission that it should not be a requirement. The exclusion of sexual infidelity as a trigger is also strange as the original defence (provocation) was developed for that type of incitement. The courts have tried to correct this injustice by a generous interpretation, as in **Clinton 2012**.

Gross negligence manslaughter has been criticised as unclear and justice requires clarity. In **Wood and Hodgson 2003**, the Ds seemed just as negligent as the caretaker in **Warner 2014**, but they were found not guilty. In **Willoughby 2004**, the judge had trouble identifying whether it was gross negligence or unlawful act manslaughter. This suggests the law is still too uncertain, as argued in **Misra 2004**. In **Khan 1998**, the CA held there was no duty to act and this type of manslaughter could not be caused by an omission. The prostitute who died did not get justice.

Task 13

Look back at the examples under the euthanasia heading in Chapter 2. Choose any case and make some notes on whether you believe justice was achieved. Then add a theorist or two, noting whether they would agree with you or not.

Generally, criminal law achieves justice by grading crimes and providing for a maximum sentence based on the seriousness of the offence. Thus theft carries a maximum of 7 years but robbery carries a maximum life sentence because of the use of violence. The non-fatal offences fail in this respect because GBH under **s 20** carries the same maximum as ABH, despite the higher level of harm. In addition, a criticism of the possible life sentence for robbery is that the force may be really minor, as in **Corcoran 1980** and **Clouden 1987**.

Theft is a crime whatever is stolen, so if a mother steals milk for her baby she is still guilty of theft. Some people may think the law is unjust, although everyone is being treated equally. However, if each case is decided on its own facts it creates uncertainty. Justice may be better achieved during the sentencing stage, rather than by deciding it is not theft. Alternatively, the **Ghosh 1982** test allows the jury to decide what standards to judge D by. Thus a jury may decide D is not guilty based on a moral perception of right and wrong rather than by following the strict letter of the law.

As regards attempted crimes, the CA recognised in **Pace and Rogers 2014** that the courts *"do not always reveal a consistency in approach"*. This shows that the **Criminal Attempts Act** has not sufficiently clarified the law on this area. It thus fails to achieve justice, because justice requires the law to be both clear and accessible.

Any of the defences can be discussed with justice because they are an attempt to balance the benefits and burdens by taking the circumstances into account.

The defence of necessity is rare, but is based on the utilitarian concept of the greater good. In **Re A (conjoined twins) 2000**, the operation to separate conjoined twins (Mary and Jodie) would lead to the death of Mary. Without the operation both twins would die, so it could be argued that her death was justified to bring about the 'greater good' of life for Jodie. The operation was allowed. The opening quote came from this case, recognising that justice means different things to different people.

In **Brown 1994,** on consent to harm, Lord Lowry said sadomasochism was *"not conducive to the welfare of society"*, so a utilitarian might agree with the verdict. The rights of the individuals to consent to harm were outweighed by the effect on society. This goes against the idea of personal autonomy and the libertarian view of justice.

3.6 Justice and contract law

The law tries to achieve a balance between allowing people freedom to make agreements in their own way and protecting the individual against those with more power, who may try to exploit this freedom. Terms are implied into contracts by both statutes (e.g., the **Consumer Rights Act 2015**) and the courts (e.g., **The Moorcock**) to protect weaker parties. Unfair terms are also regulated by the **Consumer Rights Act** which brings together several earlier laws on contract terms. This is distributive justice as it is an attempt to balance the burdens and benefits fairly between businesses and consumers.

Innominate terms, as seen in **Hong Kong Fir 1962**, are an attempt to achieve justice by focusing on the result of a breach, rather than on the term itself.

In deciding whether something is a term or a representation, the courts will take into account any specialist knowledge in order to do justice to both parties (**Oscar Chess Ltd 1957**).

Equity is based on fairness and can be seen as a higher source of law. Thus, equitable remedies, such as rescission, will only be granted if injustice won't be caused.

3.7 Justice and the law of tort

The third part of the **Caparo** test, which developed the principles from **Donoghue v Stevenson 1932** on when to impose a duty of care, is an attempt to achieve justice. Looking at what is fair, just and reasonable allows the judge to consider the circumstances and do what is fair depending on the facts of the case. In **Hill v CC of West Yorkshire 1988**, the police owed no duty of care because it could detract from their overall effectiveness. The individual's right (to damages) was outweighed by the benefit to the public. This is a utilitarian argument.

In **Miller v Jackson 1977**, the utility argument can also be seen. The public benefit of cricket outweighed the individual nuisance and no injunction was granted.

Rylands v Fletcher 1868 is a tort of strict liability, which makes a person liable without proof of fault. This can be seen as unjust.

The decision that a learner driver is expected to reach the standard of a competent driver could be seen as unjust in **Nettleship v Weston 1971**. However, the driver was best able to bear the cost, through her insurance company, so it is perhaps a fair distribution of burdens.

The defence of contributory negligence allows the court to apportion liability in a way that seeks to achieve justice. Use any cases on this defence to discuss this. One example is **Belka v Prosperini 2011**, where C had drunk about four pints of beer and was hit by a taxi while he and a friend were crossing a dual carriageway near a roundabout. He claimed in negligence for his injuries. The court found that both the taxi-driver and C were to blame. Justice was achieved by apportioning blame so that C received compensation, but this was reduced according to his level of fault. Similarly, in **Sedge**

v Prime 2011, C had been drinking and stepped out onto a narrow road without looking. He was hit by a car and suffered serious injuries. The driver was found to be in breach of his duty of care to a pedestrian because he was in a 20 mph limit zone where there were several pubs and fast-food outlets, and it was 'turning out' time for the pubs. The driver was found to be 75% responsible. Justice here was achieved by finding the driver mostly responsible because his was the greater fault, but also finding that C had a 25% share of the blame because had he looked he would have seen the car.

Also on defences, consent is only available where it is real consent, thus in **Smith v Baker 1891**, the court achieved justice by protecting the weaker party (the employee) and finding there was no true consent.

Task 14

Look back at the examples under the morality and tort heading in Chapter 2. Choose any case and make some notes on whether you believe justice was achieved. Then add a theorist or two, noting whether they would agree with you or not.

3.8 Justice and human rights

As the aim of the **ECHR** is to protect fundamental freedoms, it is designed to achieve justice. Look back to the morality and human rights section in Chapter 2 for some examples but this time focus on whether the law is achieving or promoting justice. Other examples include:

Article 2 – the right to life. Any murder or manslaughter cases can illustrate the right to life, as can the euthanasia cases in the previous chapter. Cases where a life is in danger are also illustrative and include people seeking asylum in another country. In **HJ (Iran) v Home Department 2010**, the Supreme Court ruled that gay and lesbian asylum seekers should not be forced to return to a country where they will be persecuted. **A 2** was relevant because the penalty in Iran was execution. The Government had said that they could avoid persecution by pretending to be heterosexual. The Supreme Court said that although the **ECHR** did not protect this type of persecution specifically, the decision denied them their fundamental rights to be who they are.

Article 6 – the right to a fair trial. The **Protection of Freedoms Act 2012** reduces the detention of terrorist suspects to a maximum of 14 days without charge. At one time suspects could be locked up indefinitely. This led the Law Society to say that although it was important that terror legislation protects the country, it should do so *"without compromising the government's duty to uphold fairness and justice"*. Lord Hoffman said that terrorism had succeeded if it meant the country rejected the rule of law in response to threats of terrorism. Justice requires adherence to the rule of law and although people want to be safe most do not want to live in a society that can lock people up without charge. The **Act** also provides that fingerprint and DNA evidence must be destroyed following a decision not to charge or an acquittal in court. These issues had often been cited as unjust and have been the subject of various campaigns and protests.

Article 8 – the right to a private and family life. For examples of cases under **A 8** look at the issue of data protection in the previous chapter. The judges in the **Watson** case identified two main issues with the UK law on data protection, despite several different Acts being passed since the EU directive in 1995. Firstly, it did not provide for independent scrutiny to ensure any collection or retention of data was necessary and secondly, it did not make clear what amounted to 'serious crime'. Justice requires the law to be both accessible and clear.

There are more examples in Chapter 5 as judges have to balance competing interests in order to achieve justice.

Task 15

Look back at the examples under the morality and human rights and/or technology headings in Chapter 2. Choose any case and make some notes on whether you believe justice was achieved. Then add a theorist or two, noting whether they would agree with you or not.

Examination tip

Read the question carefully. Examination questions are designed to stretch and challenge you so will change the focus each time. You may be asked to consider a law or procedure and to discuss whether it *achieves* justice. You may be asked how far a law or procedure *promotes* justice. In each case you will first need an explanation of justice (with reference to some of the theories), then you need to address the 'achieve' or 'promote' part of the question.

If the word 'achieve' is used you need to consider whether the result is just. This can be in your opinion but use a theorist or two to support what you say and case examples to illustrate. If the word 'promote' is used, you will need to consider the way the law can promote justice. For example, Parliament can attempt to *promote* justice when making the legal rules by regulating how people behave. In contract and tort, the **Consumer Rights Act** gives protection to consumers by regulating how manufacturers and retailers behave. In tort, the **Occupier's Liability Act 1984** protects people by imposing a duty on an occupier to keep the premises safe for people even though they have no right to be there. It was the attempt to do justice in **BRB v Herrington 1972** that led to this Act being passed. Similarly following the **Quintavalle** case, Parliament passed the **Human Fertilisation and Embryology Act 2008** to regulate the medical procedures. This shows that case law can also promote justice by highlighting any gaps or uncertainties in the law and encouraging the government to make changes through Parliament.

Sentencing and remedies can also promote justice, e.g., by deterrence and by making people act more carefully in future.

You can plan a basic answer explaining the theories in advance, but if the question refers to a specific law or procedure you will then need to adapt. You need to focus on the topic selected and choose your examples carefully to ensure they are relevant. It is best to avoid emotive words; examiners want to see a reasoned opinion, not a rant. Here is an example of an outline answer using a specific criminal law as a base and indicating which theories and cases can be discussed and developed. For a question linked to the legal system you would focus on the law-making aspect (statutory interpretation and precedent).

Example

Does the exclusion of sexual infidelity as a qualifying trigger under the **Coroners and Justice Act** achieve justice?

Once an explanation of justice has been provided (e.g., as based on equality and/or fairness, as based on rules, as based on morality, as based on maximising happiness etc.), the focus would be on **s 55 (6)**, with a possible reference to the old defence of provocation which had no such requirement. You could consider why the law was changed and what the purpose of **s 55 (6)** is and then whether the new law can/does achieve justice. You should refer back to your theories so that you show the examiner you understand that a law may be seen as just under one theory and unjust under another. A positivist would say the law is just if made properly so may regard it as a just law.

However, as the law is ambiguous judges will have to interpret it and may put their own values on it, as in **Brown**. Justice requires certainty in the law so the ambiguity of the law is itself a potential injustice. Natural law theory would say the law is based on morals so may see this law as unjust because it prevents someone relying on an immoral act as a trigger. A utilitarian would look at the overall benefit and may see the benefit to society in general in being protected from those who kill as more important than the defendant's rights to use the defence to avoid a life sentence.

For example cases you could refer to **Holley 2005** (when sexual infidelity could justify the loss of control for the old law of provocation) and then to cases after the law changed such as **Clinton 2012**, **Dawes 2013** and **Gurpinar 2015** to highlight the role of the courts in achieving justice by way of statutory interpretation. The purposive approach was used in **Clinton** and this set a precedent for the later cases.

3.9 Justice and public opinion

Not only do the theorists differ in their ideas of justice, so do most ordinary people. In a televised report of a court case you often see pictures of families and friends of the victim, and the accused, demanding 'justice'. Whatever the outcome of the case, they are unlikely all to think that they got it. This is illustrated by the opening quote from Ward LJ.

The case of the Libyan, Al Megrahi, convicted of the 1988 'Lockerbie bombing' over Scotland, illustrates the different ways people view 'justice'. In 2009, he was allowed by the Scottish government to return to Libya, as he was ill and expected to die within a few months. (He actually died in 2012.) The Americans who had family killed on the flight were strongly opposed to the decision to allow him to return to Libya to die, and wished to see him punished in full for his actions. The Americans wanted retributive justice. The Scottish families said they wanted a full enquiry to establish the facts of the case, as many of them remain unconvinced of his guilt. Justice to them meant ensuring that the man accused was actually guilty. An enquiry could produce new evidence and could lead to corrective justice via the CCRC.

Evaluation pointer

What do you think the families and friends actually mean when they say they want justice? Look out for stories in the press. As you read, ask yourself whether 'justice' has been achieved. Then consider whether any of the above theorists would have agreed. Finally, ask the all-important question, "justice for whom?" Write some notes on this to keep for revision.

Examination tip

Examiners are looking for independence of thought so you need to develop your own ideas. Use some of the examples but don't just cite them. Pick out a few and see how well you can explain them. Include references to some of the theories and add cases to illustrate. Hopefully, the last three tasks will help you with this.

Example

Re A is a good example of the difficulties judges face when trying to achieve justice. The parents and the doctors could not agree and nor would the theorists. A follower of natural law would want to uphold the parents' wishes, as the operation would kill one of the twins and taking a life is immoral and therefore not justice. A utilitarian would say that overall the most benefits would be achieved by the operation going ahead because at least one life would be saved, however the effect on society as a whole would need to be taken into account because it is total happiness that matters not an arithmetical number. Many people would argue that justice is better achieved by the law coming from an elected Parliament rather than from judges.

Examination tip

Try to include something recent that involves a question of promoting or achieving justice as examiners like to see new ideas and examples. There are plenty of 2016 and 2017 laws and cases here but it is a good idea to keep an eye in the media for new ones.

Summary

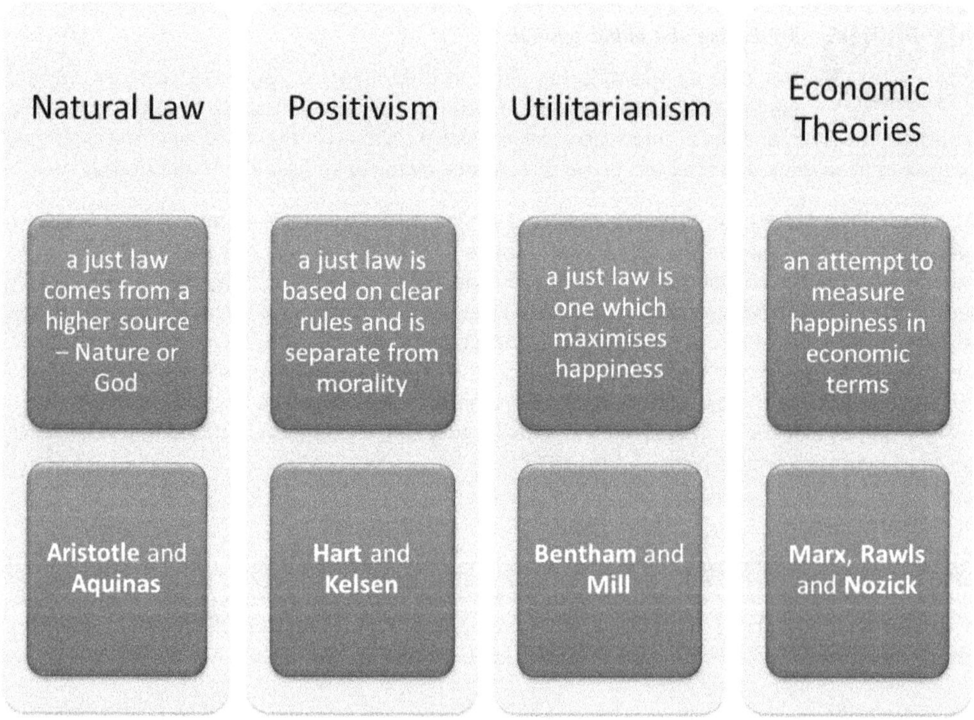
Natural Law
a just law comes from a higher source – Nature or God
Aristotle and Aquinas
Positivism
a just law is based on clear rules and is separate from morality
Hart and Kelsen
Utilitarianism
a just law is one which maximises happiness
Bentham and Mill
Economic Theories
an attempt to measure happiness in economic terms
Marx, Rawls and Nozick

Self-test questions

1. *What is the utilitarian theory based on?*
2. *What do positivists attempt to separate?*
3. *What did Mill add to utilitarianism?*
4. *Where does natural law come from?*
5. *Apply one of these theories to any case of your choice.*

For answers to the tasks and self-test questions, please go to my website at www.drsr.org and click the button 'Answers to Kindle tasks'

Chapter 4 Law and society – Fault

"Vicarious liability is a species of strict liability ... an employer who is not personally at fault is made legally answerable for the fault of his employee"

Lord Millett

By the end of this Chapter you should be able to:

- ***Explain the meaning and importance of fault in criminal liability***
- ***Explain the meaning and importance of fault in civil liability***
- ***Evaluate the role of fault and compare this to strict liability in criminal and/or civil law***

4.1 What is fault?

Fault implies a sense of blameworthiness. If you are accused of doing something you might say "but it wasn't my fault". You will usually mean that you are not to blame for it. It is a general principle of both criminal and civil law that liability is based on fault. Individual responsibility is also a general principle. However, these are principles not rules and there are exceptions.

There are three main areas to discuss in relation to fault.

- ***The importance of fault***
- ***Liability without fault (exceptions to fault-based liability)***
- ***Whether there should be liability without fault***

Examination tip

Although liability is usually based on fault, there are exceptions. You should be prepared to discuss not only the concept of fault and its importance, but also the exceptions and whether it is right to impose liability *without* proof of fault.

We'll look at these three issues in relation to criminal and civil law respectively.

4.2 The importance of fault in criminal law

Fault is very important in criminal cases because criminal wrongdoing is assumed to be a matter of individual choice. This means there is not usually criminal liability for actions outside the individual's control (this is evident in the defences of insanity, automatism, diminished responsibility and loss of control). Fault can be seen in connection with *mens rea* (the act is done intentionally, recklessly or negligently), *actus reus* (the act is done voluntarily), defences (there is no excuse or justification for the act) and sentencing (the aim of sentencing is to reflect the level of fault when committing the act). We will take these in turn and see how far the principle of no liability without fault applies in practice by looking at some cases.

Fault and *mens rea*

Most crimes require *mens rea,* so even if D has carried out a criminal act, there will be no liability unless it happened with *mens rea*. There are different levels of *mens rea,* or fault. Intent is the highest, then subjective recklessness and gross negligence.

Intent is the *mens rea* for murder and several property offences. In **Madeley 1990**, the TV show host was not guilty of theft as he was able to show he was suffering from stress and merely forgot to pay for the goods. He did not intend to avoid paying. Theft also requires dishonesty and **s 2** of the **Theft Act** provides three situations where D will not be found dishonest and so will not be guilty of theft even though appropriating another's property. If D has an honest belief that the property could be taken for one of the three reasons there is a lower level of fault so this seems fair.

In the most serious crime, murder, D may be guilty even if there is only intent to seriously injure (**DPP v Smith 1960**). This is a lower level of fault than intent to kill, but the result is the same, a life sentence. As we saw with justice, the correspondence principle requires that the *mens rea* and *actus reus* of a crime should match. Where this doesn't happen, called constructive liability, there is a lower level of *mens rea* (fault). Constructive liability also applies to involuntary manslaughter and two of the non-fatal offences against the person. In all these cases the level of fault is less than the offences seem to require. D should only be liable where fully blameworthy for the crime, i.e., with the *mens rea* for the offence actually committed.

Subjective recklessness involves finding that D recognised the risk of the consequence, but went ahead anyway. Thus in **Cunningham 1957,** the prosecution failed to prove that D was aware his actions might cause harm, so he did not have the required level of fault to be found guilty.

In **Jones v First-tier Tribunal 2011**, D had run in front of a lorry and it had been held at trial that he had no *mens rea* as he had only intended to harm himself, not anyone else. On appeal the CA disagreed and held that he must have recognised harm could be caused to the driver of the lorry, so had the *mens rea* of recklessness. He was therefore held to be guilty of inflicting grievous bodily harm. This was more like objective than subjective recklessness and so a low level of fault for a serious crime. The decision was reversed by the Supreme Court in **Jones v FTT 2013**. The SC reinstated the tribunal's decision that there was no *mens rea* and held it was not enough that anyone running into a busy road must have seen the risk of some harm, as the CA had decided. It was whether D himself foresaw the risk of harm. This was a matter for the tribunal and not an appeal court.

At one time, there was also objective recklessness. When the HL, in **Gemmell & Richards 2003**, overruled **Caldwell 1982** and abolished objective recklessness, they recognised the injustice of finding D guilty where there was a low level of fault, i.e., where D did not recognise a risk of the consequence but a reasonable person would have done. A case where the old law was particularly unfair was **Elliot 1983**, where she had no idea of the possible consequences of her actions but was found guilty of criminal damage by fire.

Constructive liability as discussed above also applies to two offences requiring a *mens rea* of recklessness, ABH under **s 47 Offences against the Person Act** and GBH under **s 20**. As with murder and manslaughter, the level of fault does not match the act. Case examples include **Roberts 1971**, **Savage 1991** and **Mowatt 1968**.

Gross negligence is the fault element for manslaughter. In **Wacker 2003**, the Ds were transporting illegal immigrants in a lorry with no ventilation and most died. In finding them guilty of gross negligence manslaughter the judge referred to **Adomako 1994** and the *"ordinary principles of the law of negligence"*. It seems wrong that the civil rules on duty of care are applied to a serious crime. Negligence may be sufficient fault for civil law, but it is arguable that for crimes there should be at least subjective recklessness.

Once a duty is established, whether D's conduct was sufficiently grossly negligent for criminal (rather than civil) liability is for the jury to decide. This was stated in **Adomako** and confirmed in **Misra 2004**. This may be difficult, and different juries may come to different decisions on how much 'fault' D has shown.

Example

Comparing two cases from the previous chapter highlights this problem.

In **Wood and Hodgson 2003**, a 10-year-old girl was visiting the Ds. She found some ecstasy tablets hidden in a cigarette packet and took some. After some delay they eventually called an ambulance but she later died in hospital. The jury decided that they had not shown a sufficiently high level of negligence to be deemed criminal and found them not guilty of gross negligence manslaughter.

In **Warner 2014**, a caretaker failed to replace a gap in the barrier of a walkway and a child fell to her death. The judge said his failure to replace the barrier had been *"thoroughly irresponsible"*. The jury found him guilty of gross negligence manslaughter.

It can be argued that Wood and Hodgson were also thoroughly irresponsible so the cases are hard to reconcile.

Another case which illustrates the relationship between fault and crime is **Khan 1998**. In this case there was a high level of fault because they knew she might die but did nothing to help. It seems wrong that with that level of fault they were not guilty. Again, this can be compared to **Warner** where the man was merely careless but was guilty of manslaughter. These cases illustrate the fact that the level of fault involved can vary enormously from something just short of intent to kill to the virtually accidental.

The other type of manslaughter also illustrates the problems with fault and constructive liability. Unlawful act manslaughter has a *mens rea* of intent or subjective recklessness, but this is only required for the unlawful act, not for the death.

Example

In a case like **Nedrick 1986**, where the unlawful act is arson (a form of criminal damage), it is only necessary to show that D intends or recognises a risk of damage by fire, not death or serious injury. In the case, he poured paraffin through V's letterbox so arson was clearly intended. *Mens rea* is therefore easy to prove for a manslaughter charge to succeed. This seems a low level of fault for a serious crime but was seen again in **JF 2015**. The Ds were teenagers who had set fire to an old duvet in a derelict building. The fire spread and a homeless man was killed by the fumes. The unlawful act was again arson with the *mens rea* of intent or recklessness to cause damage by fire. They had intended the fire (and the fire caused the death) so were convicted of manslaughter. The conviction was upheld on appeal. In this case, the level of fault was even lower because they were just boys.

The fault element in attempted crimes can be criticised as not achieving justice. This relates to both *mens rea* and *actus reus*. In **Geddes 1996**, he was not guilty because he had not approached any victim, but there was clear evidence of his intentions and so a high level of fault. In **Campbell 1991**, the act was not 'more than merely preparatory' so he was not guilty. The problem is that if the police wait until the act is more than preparatory before arresting D, they could be putting people in danger. Also with attempt, the fault element is often higher than the relevant conduct suggests, unlike constructive liability where it is lower. This means D is not criminally liable for an attempted crime unless there is specific intent to commit it, even if the offence itself can be committed recklessly. An example case to illustrate this is **Millard & Vernon 1987** where the Ds had been reckless but were not guilty of attempted criminal damage as intent could not be proved.

It is the role of law to protect the public and this is clearly an issue with attempted crimes as there are so many not guilty verdicts in cases where there is a high level of fault.

Similarly, for attempted murder there must be intent to kill, but murder itself only requires intent seriously to injure. So the full offence requires a lower level of fault than the attempted one. A person charged with attempted murder may be found not guilty where, had the victim died and the charge been murder, it would have been a guilty verdict. This seems wrong as it may be that someone who intends to kill and so has a high level of fault is not guilty of a crime merely because the victim is tough or has speedy medical treatment. This applies to quick reactions too, as in **Z 2017**, where the victim only avoided death by her fast response to the attack. As it happens in that case, D was guilty of attempted murder because the jury found intent to kill, but the point remains that liability is not sufficiently connected to the level of fault.

Fault and actus reus

Although *mens rea* is the main fault element in criminal law, *actus reus* also relates to fault. The rule is that D's actions must be voluntary, thus there was no conviction for failing to stop at a pedestrian crossing in **Leicester v Pearson 1952,** because D was pushed onto the crossing by another car; he was not at fault.

Evaluation pointer

D can be liable for *failing* to do something, which doesn't seem as blameworthy as actively doing something. In **Pittwood 1902**, the gatekeeper forgot to close the gate and was guilty of manslaughter when someone was killed by a train. As well as **Warner**, discussed above, there are many other case examples on omissions which can be used to illustrate that a low level of fault may be enough for a manslaughter conviction.

Causation also has a connection with fault. There will be no liability if D did not cause the result, so if the victim or a third party does something which breaks the chain of causation D is not to blame for the result. D may be at fault in respect of a lesser crime, but not the one that resulted. In **Kennedy 2007**, D had committed an unlawful act in supplying the heroin, but the victim's act in self-administering the drug broke the chain of causation. D did not cause death so he was not guilty of manslaughter, only of the lesser crime of supplying illegal drugs. On the other hand, if someone acts foreseeably the chain is not broken so D is liable for the full consequences, even if not intended or foreseen. This seems harsh, as can be seen in **Roberts 1971**, where no harm was intended or foreseen, but he was liable for ABH. The thin skull rule also seems harsh because there may be liability for consequences completely unforeseen by D, as in **Blaue 1975**. On the other hand, in that case, D had a high level of fault because he stabbed her several times so it can be argued that he should be liable for all the consequences.

Task 16

Using three cases you know, explain the fault element and how this affected whether or not D was found guilty of an offence.

Fault and defences

One role of the law is to protect both individuals and society as a whole and another is to do this based on the level of blameworthiness involved. Most defences are examples of this relationship between liability and fault. The fault element can be removed or mitigated by the defences. Defences such as insanity show a reduced level of fault in that D is not fully responsible. If D has a defect of reason, and does not realise that an act is legally wrong, then there is a low degree of fault. In such cases, the role of law should not be to punish but to protect, e.g., a hospital order may be appropriate and this will protect both D and the wider public. The judge has discretion in which order to make so can take into account the level of fault. Automatism shows no fault at all as D does not have control over the act committed. In **Hill v Baxter 1958**, a hypothetical example was given of D being attacked by a swarm of bees whilst driving a car. If this caused a total loss of control, the automatism defence would succeed. This total lack of fault is reflected in the result. A successful plea of automatism means an acquittal. However, the law on insanity and automatism is not always consistent. It can hardly be said that a person is at fault when sleepwalking (**Burgess 1991**) or during an epileptic fit (**Sullivan 1984**). However, in the first case D was given a secure hospital order and in the second changed his plea to guilty to avoid the insanity verdict and was convicted of ABH.

Duress and self-defence show a reduced level of fault, although they *excuse* rather than remove it. D is not saying, *"I did it but it wasn't my fault"* but *"I did it but had good reason to do so"*. One role of law is to protect so it is right that duress should not apply to murder. However, if D is forced to act because of a serious threat of harm, or even death, the lower level of fault cannot be taken into account. This is because the sentence for murder is mandatory life imprisonment and we have seen the problems with this earlier. Intoxication may remove fault if D is involuntarily intoxicated and cannot form intent. Voluntary intoxication reduces the level of fault if the *mens rea* is intent only, and any conviction will be for the lesser crime, e.g., manslaughter not murder or **s 20** not **s 18**. However, the defence of intoxication rarely succeeds unless it completely removes the required fault element. Thus D was found guilty in **Kingston 1994**. If the *mens rea* includes recklessness, D is seen to be reckless, and thus at fault, in getting drunk (**Majewski 1977**). It is arguable that being reckless in getting drunk is not the same as being reckless as to committing an assault, but in **Majewski**, the HL held that it supplied sufficient evidence of *mens rea* for the charge of ABH.

The partial defences both reflect a lower level of fault. If successful, they reduce murder to manslaughter thus allowing the judge to choose an appropriate sentence that reflects the level of fault. Any of the cases of voluntary manslaughter can be used to illustrate this (see also under sentencing below). The law recognises that D is not fully blameworthy in some circumstances. If D suffered from diminished responsibility, as in **Freaney 2011**, where she was suffering extreme stress when she killed her son, the conviction is reduced from murder to manslaughter. The **Coroners and Justice Act** has improved the law but problems remain. The Law Commission recommended that developmental immaturity in those under 18 should be included within the definition of diminished responsibility as a recognised medical condition. This is because the parts of the brain which play an important role in the development of self-control do not mature until 14 years of age. The **CJA** did not take up this proposal so a child who kills will be treated in the same way as an adult, even though there is a lower level of fault. The conviction is also reduced from murder to manslaughter where D suffers a loss of control, as long as there is a valid trigger, as in **Clinton 2012** and **Gurpinar 2015**. Any other cases where either defence succeeded can be used to illustrate the importance of fault in criminal liability. The success of the defence indicates that there is a reason for the killing, and thus a lower level of fault. The reduction to manslaughter allows the judge discretion, so any fault can be taken into account when sentencing, which brings us to the last point.

Fault and sentencing

At the final stage of a criminal case the sentence given will reflect the level of fault. Mitigating and aggravating factors are taken into account, so if the circumstances indicate a higher or lower level of fault this is reflected in the sentence. One problem is the mandatory life sentence for murder, which means the judge cannot take into account any lack of moral fault, e.g., in euthanasia cases. All a judge can do to reflect the level of fault is recommend a starting point or a maximum term, but this is a limited discretion. An example is the case of **Inglis 2010**, where the circumstances were similar to **Freaney 2011** but she failed in her plea of diminished responsibility. She was given a life sentence for murder, but with a starting point of 9 years rather than the usual 15, on compassionate grounds.

As discussed with defences, where the partial defences are successful and the judge has discretion, the level of fault can be reflected in the sentence.

The role of law is to punish those at fault. The grading of offences and maximum sentences both take into account the level of fault. This may not seem just with certain non-fatal offences, e.g., the sentencing for ABH and reckless GBH is the same. Wounding with intent and robbery more fairly reflect the level of fault. There is a higher degree of fault seen in the intent to cause serious harm and the intentional use or threat of force, so for both these crimes the maximum punishment goes up to life imprisonment. One criticism of this possible sentence for robbery is that the amount of force may be very small, as in **Corcoran 1980** and **Clouden 1987**. If someone uses minimum force there is less fault than when someone attacks with a weapon. However, as this sentence is not mandatory the judge can take the level of fault into account when sentencing.

As regards sentencing generally, it can be argued that the imposition of sanctions and any restriction on the freedom of the individual is only justified when that individual has been at fault.

The aims of sentencing can also be discussed in relation to fault. The role of the law is to punish those who are blameworthy, so one aim of sentencing is to make the sentence fit the crime. Murder has a very high degree of fault so a life sentence is usually justified. A deterrent sentence is less justified because it often sacrifices the interests of the individual to those of society, rather than reflecting the level of fault involved. It is used to stop re-offending and deter others from offending, so a custodial sentence may be given where the offence does not really warrant one.

Evaluation pointer

Here are a few points which can be developed in an evaluation of fault:

Consider how much real fault there is in cases involving omissions.

The degree of fault in murder cases may be very different, but the result is the same – a life sentence. You could compare the level of fault in a vicious murder to that in euthanasia cases.

Constructive liability applies to murder, manslaughter and two non-fatal offences. D should only be liable where the *mens rea* was for the offence actually committed but in the following crimes D can be liable for an offence which is more serious:

> Murder only requires intent to commit serious harm not to kill.
>
> Unlawful act manslaughter only requires that D has *mens rea* for the act, not for the death.
>
> ABH under **s 47** only requires the *mens rea* for an assault or a battery.
>
> GBH under **s 20** only requires the *mens rea* for 'some harm', not serious harm.

In all these cases there is a lower level of fault than the offence warrants. This constructive liability seems unjust.

Task 17

Look at the above evaluation pointer and add a case or two to each point

Some crimes do not require *mens rea* in any form. Liability without fault is called *strict* liability. You should already have studied this but more evaluation is needed now. You may have to consider how far someone *should* be criminally liable without proof of fault. As always, there are arguments on both sides. A quick recap:

4.3 Liability without fault in criminal law

Strict liability usually applies to regulatory offences, i.e., offences that are not truly criminal in nature such as minor traffic offences. In addition, offences covering areas of social concern or public health are often strict liability offences.

Examples

Examples include health and safety (**Gammon (Hong Kong) Ltd v AG of HK 1985**), the sale of food and alcohol (**Meah v Roberts 1977**), and pollution and protection of the environment (**Alphacell v Woodward 1972**).

In **Meah v Roberts 1977**, D served lemonade which had caustic soda in it to two children. She was not responsible for it being there, but was found guilty under the **Food and Drug Act 1955**, even though not at fault.

Underage gambling is also seen as a matter of social concern. In **Harrow LBC v Shah 1999,** it was held that the offence of selling a lottery ticket to a person under 16 was one of strict liability so D was guilty even though staff had been properly instructed. In 'real' crimes there is more controversy, as seen in **Sweet v Parsley 1970**. A woman let rooms to students and the police raided the premises and found cannabis. She was charged with being *"concerned in the management of premises used for the purpose of smoking cannabis"* under the **Dangerous Drugs Act 1965**. She was found guilty even though not at fault – she was completely unaware of the cannabis smoking. The HL eventually acquitted her and established the rule that strict liability could only be imposed where the Act specifically made the offence one of strict liability. Guidelines for the imposition of liability without fault were set out in **Gammon (Hong Kong) Ltd v AG of HK 1985** as follows:

- there is a presumption that *mens rea* is required
- the presumption is particularly strong if the offence is 'truly' criminal
- the presumption can only be displaced if the statute clearly states or implies that *mens rea* is not required
- the presumption can only be displaced if the statute deals with an issue of social concern and public safety is an issue

As you can see, these build on the principle of **Sweet v Parsley** but make clear the presumption that *mens rea* is required can only be displaced if the Act is clear and the case involves a matter of social concern. In all other cases, a need for *mens rea* will be presumed.

In **B v DPP 2000**, the HL reversed a conviction of inciting a child of 14 to indecency on the basis of this principle, saying it was particularly strong in serious offences. D had argued he was not at fault as he believed the child was older. For 'real' crimes such as this, particularly where a prison sentence may result, it is important that *mens rea* should be proved. This was again made clear in two SC cases where **Sweet v Parsley** was referred to.

In **Hughes 2013**, D was charged with causing death by driving while uninsured and unlicensed under the **Road Traffic Act 1988 as amended**. The CA accepted that this was a strict liability offence but the SC held that there must be some element of fault in the driving which contributed to the death. The other driver had been 100% at fault and it would be wrong to blame Hughes for the death. Referring to **Sweet v Parsley**, the SC pointed out that this was not a regulatory offence, it carried a possible prison sentence and involved serious social stigma. As regards causation, the words 'by driving' indicated that the offence required some element of fault even if it was only a flat tyre. Parliament could have used different words to make it clear if it was to be a strict liability offence.

The decision was followed in **Taylor 2016**. D took a car without consent and collided with a scooter. The scooter rider later died and D was charged with aggravated vehicle taking (**Theft Act s 12A**) and with causing a death while uninsured (**Road Traffic Act 1988**). Aggravated vehicle taking includes taking a vehicle and then either driving dangerously or causing injury 'owing to the driving'. The prosecution argued that *mens rea* was only needed as regards the taking of the vehicle and nothing more. The SC rejected this argument and held that there had to be some act or omission in the control of the car which involved an element of fault and contributed to the death. The fact that he had taken the car without consent was not enough, because the taking of the car did not cause the death. These cases show the reluctance of the courts to impose strict liability unless the Act is clear that fault is not required.

Some statutes specifically provide a defence to strict liability crimes where D can prove that all due care was taken. This is known as the 'due diligence' defence and indicates a lack of fault. An example is the **Licensing Act 2003** which provides a defence to various offences under the Act, such as selling alcohol to young people, if D *"exercised all due diligence to avoid committing the offence"*. The Act must be clear that a defence is allowed and the courts will not find such a defence unless Parliament specifically provides for it, as seen in **Harrow LBC v Shah 1999**. The **National Lottery Regulations** had no such provision so he was guilty even though care had been taken.

The Law Commission suggested in a 2010 report that Parliament should state more clearly whether an offence was one of strict liability or not. This seems a sensible way forward but has not yet been seen in practice.

Some crimes do not require any fault at all. These are 'state of affairs' crimes where D can be liable just for being in the wrong place at the wrong time, as in **Larsonneur 1933**. In **Winzar 1983**, a drunk was removed from a hospital by the police and put in their car, which was parked on the road. They then arrested him for being found 'drunk on a highway', and he was convicted. Here there is not only no *mens rea* but no *actus reus*, as he was not acting voluntarily.

Evaluation pointer

State of affairs crimes such as **Larsonneur** and **Winzar** mean D can be liable without being at fault, or even acting voluntarily. This seems unfair.

4.4 Whether there should be liability without fault in criminal law

Arguments against:

- ***it is unfair to convict D of a criminal offence if not at fault***
- ***it leads to the punishment of people who have taken all possible precautions***
- ***it means such people have a criminal record***

Arguments for:

- ***it makes people more careful***
- ***it protects the public***
- ***most such offences are minor and carry no social stigma***
- ***proving mens rea is hard in many minor offences, e.g., trying to prove someone knew they had parked on a yellow line in the snow, so time and money is saved***

- ***the judge can address the issue of fault when sentencing***

Although there are several arguments for imposing strict liability, the arguments against are very strong. A requirement of fault, at least negligence, would seem fairer. This is a low level of fault so would still protect the public, but it would mean there would be no conviction without some degree of fault.

Task 18

Choose a case from criminal law and one from civil law. Choose one argument for and one against strict liability and develop them using the case in support of what you say. This will help you produce a balanced argument.

Examination tip

Use cases you are familiar with from whatever area of law you have studied to illustrate an answer. Some of the ideas here could also be considered in a discussion of law and justice so make a note of those where you feel justice has not been achieved.

4.5 The importance of fault in civil law

Fault is an element of many areas of civil law. It is seen in contract but is particularly important in tort. The word negligence itself implies a degree of fault.

Contract law

Fault is, perhaps, less important in contract cases. The fact of breach is enough and there is no need, e.g., to prove negligence. However, the party in breach is seen as the one at fault, and so damages are awarded to the other party. Any breach cases can be used to illustrate the concept. Also, if the breach is fundamental the injured party can not only claim damages but can also treat the contract as at an end, reflecting the higher level of fault.

Misrepresentation usually relies on proving fraud or negligence. Fraud is a high level of fault. In **Derry v Peek 1889**, it was described as where a false statement was made *knowingly*, without belief in its truth, or *recklessly*, careless as to whether it is true or false. Negligence is a lower level of fault in that it can include a statement which was honestly made, as in **Howard Marine and Dredging Ltd 1978,** where D was at fault, or negligent, in not checking the information.

Evaluation pointer

Since the **Misrepresentation Act,** an action for innocent misrepresentation is possible. Here there is no fault. Do you think this is fair to D?

The law on frustration reflects the fact that where neither of the parties to a contract are at fault in ending it, neither can enforce it against the other. In **Davis Contractors 1956** Lord Radcliffe said "*frustration occurs whenever the law recognises that, **without default** of either party, a contractual obligation has become incapable of being performed*". So it is only where neither party could foresee an event that the event can frustrate the contract. If one party could foresee it, or is at fault, the contract will not be frustrated, e.g., **Super Servant II 1990**.

Contract remedies will reflect the degree of fault by the party in breach. Damages are only awarded for foreseeable loss, as established in **Hadley 1854**. Also, rescission is a discretionary remedy, and will not be awarded to a party who has not acted equitably, i.e., who is at fault.

Tort law

Proving D has been negligent means proving a breach of a duty of care, either at common law or under the **Occupier's Liability Acts.** For the tort of nuisance C must prove unreasonable interference with enjoyment of land. In other words, C must prove that D is *at fault*. A general principle of tort is that of individual responsibility, so there is not usually liability for matters beyond the individual's control. This can be seen in defences such as act of God, or act of a stranger. We will take these in turn and see how far the principle of no liability without fault applies in practice by looking at some cases.

Fault and negligence / occupiers' liability

The law of tort requires that people take care not to harm others. The common law on negligence stems from **Donoghue v Stevenson 1932** where it was established that a person can be liable for foreseeable harm. The manufacture was at fault for not ensuring the bottles were free of snails (or any other harmful material). A duty to take care is only imposed where harm is foreseeable. An example is **Topp v London County Bus Ltd 1993**, where the bus company was found not liable as it was not foreseeable that someone would steal the bus. The company was not at fault. For cases of psychiatric harm and economic loss the rules on proving a duty of care are stricter because it is recognised that a huge number of people may be affected, so a higher degree of fault is required. The topic that most involves fault is breach of duty. Breach means D has not taken sufficient care, i.e., has not reached the standard of a reasonable person. You can use any breach of duty cases to discuss the importance of proving fault. Note that D is judged by the standard expected of the reasonable person, not D's own standards. However, it is recognised that in the case of children, age is relevant and they should have a higher degree of fault before being found negligent, as in **Mullin v Richards 1998**. Also note that breach of duty applies to both negligence and occupiers' liability in the same way so cases from both areas can be used when discussing fault and breach.

In **Orchard v Lee 2009**, a supervisor in a school playground was injured when a thirteen-year-old child playing a game of tag ran into her. The CA held that the question was whether the conduct of the child was culpable (blameworthy), i.e., had fallen below the standard that should objectively be expected of a child of that age. The CA held that to be at fault the conduct must be "*careless to a very high degree*". As he was in a play area and was not breaking any rules he was held not to be at fault; it was merely an accident.

In professional cases, D is judged against others in the profession. In the case of doctors, against what other doctors would do. Thus if there is an error of judgment the court will consider whether others in the same area of expertise might have done the same thing (**Bolam 1957/Bolitho 1997**). Professionals are seen as more blameworthy if they do not follow normal practice, so are likely to be found in breach of duty. However, the normal breach factors still apply. In **McDonnell v Holwerda 2003,** a GP examined a child twice. The court held that not recognising the risk of meningitis on the first occasion was not negligent, but the risk was foreseeable and so higher by the second examination. The GP therefore had breached her duty on this occasion, reflecting the higher level of fault. A non-professional is regarded as less blameworthy and is compared to someone reasonably competent doing the same work. Thus in **Wells v Cooper 1958** a man was not liable for harm caused by his poor DIY carpentry work as he was judged against the standards of a reasonably competent carpenter, not a professional carpenter

The factors the courts consider when deciding if the standard has been reached also relate to fault. If there is only a low risk of something happening and precautions have been taken to avoid the risk,

D is less likely to be found at fault, as in **Bolton v Stone 1951** and **Latimer v AEC 1953**. Perfection is not required and there is no liability if the result was not foreseeable. In addition, if there is a social benefit then even if at fault D may escape liability, as in the case of **Watts v Herts CC 1954** where the fire crew were on their way to rescue someone. This is strengthened by the **Compensation Act 2006 s 1,** which provides that in deciding whether D should have taken particular steps to meet the standard of care (e.g., take precautions), a court may consider whether a requirement to take those steps might prevent a 'desirable activity' from being undertaken. This means a higher level of fault may be acceptable when the activity in question is desirable, such as school trips and sporting events.

Another aspect of fault is related to whether the breach caused the harm. **The Wagon Mound 1961** test asks whether it was foreseeable that the damage would occur. Thus D is only liable for the foreseeable consequences of any breach of duty, which reflects the level of fault better than the earlier case of **Re Polemis** where there was liability for all direct consequences of the breach. The thin skull rule applies in civil law as well as in crime and again can seem harsh because it seems to go against the rule that D is only liable for foreseeable damage (foreseeability applies to duty, breach and causation remember). There may be liability for completely unexpected consequences, as in **Smith v Leech-Brain 1961**, where an employer was liable for the death of an employee. The employer may have been at fault, because his negligence caused the burn, but his blameworthiness did not seem sufficiently high to make him liable for the death.

In occupiers' liability cases breach applies in the same way as for common law negligence. However, there are additional rules which limit the duty, especially as regards trespassers. Fault can be discussed in relation to the provisions on liability for independent contractors under the **Occupiers Liability Act 1957**. A comparison of **Haseldine v Daw 1941** with **Woodward v Mayor of Hastings 1944** illustrates the lower level of fault in the former case, where no duty was owed. The difference in **Woodward** was that the work was easy to check so the occupier was at fault for not doing this.

Both the **Occupiers Liability Act 1957** and **1984** make liability stricter in the case of children. It is right that the council was found at fault in **Glasgow Corporation v Taylor 1922** as more care should be taken to protect children from danger. It was arguably also fair in **Jolley v Sutton LBC 2000**. Where children are likely to be present or may be attracted by an allurement an occupier is more blameworthy for not keeping the area safe. However, the older the young person is, the less likely a duty will be owed. This can be illustrated by several swimming cases such as **Tomlinson 2003** and **Ratcliff v McConnell 1999**.

The principle that there is no need to warn of obvious risks and there is no duty where the injury derives from the dangerous nature of a voluntary activity rather than the state of the premises (both confirmed in **Tomlinson**) further protects the occupier. These principles recognise that in these situations C is more at fault so D is not liable.

Evaluation pointer

In **Nettleship v Weston 1971**, it was said that a learner driver should show the skill of an ordinary, competent driver. Do you think a learner driver is showing the same degree of fault as an experienced 'competent driver' would be when driving negligently?

Task 19

Choose a case from civil law (breach of contract or breach of a duty of care). Note the element of fault and how it affected liability.

Fault and nuisance

In nuisance cases it must be shown that D's act was unreasonable. This is a lesser degree of fault than negligence. In **Adams v Ursell 1818,** smells from D's fish and chip shop were unreasonable even though he was providing a service, and arguably not doing anything wrong. A higher level of fault was seen in **Christie v Davey 1893**. Both neighbours were causing a nuisance to each other, but D was liable because his behaviour was malicious and more clearly unreasonable. This suggests that although motive is not usually relevant in either criminal or civil law, the higher level of fault involved may tip the balance as to which neighbour is liable in such cases. The defence of prescription in nuisance cases means that even if D is at fault, if the nuisance has been going on for twenty years here is no liability. However, this defence only applies from the time the nuisance starts, not the time the activity starts. This can lead to an arguably unjust result. It seems wrong that D has to pay compensation in a case like **Sturges v Bridgman 1879**, where there was no nuisance until C 'came to the nuisance', in this case by moving his surgery.

Fault and defences and remedies

Tort defences may be used to argue either a total lack of fault, or reduced fault.

Example

You come home very late one night and are told you cannot go out in the evening for a week as a punishment. The reason you are late is that a bolt of lightning hit the bus you were in, causing severe delays. You would argue that this was an act of God, and you should not be punished because you were not at fault in any way.

This special defence of act of God means that if D is not at fault in any way there is no liability. It applies in nuisance, but only if D did not know of the danger. It is more often seen in **Rylands**, even though it is a tort of strict, or no fault, liability. Thus liability may be strict, but is not absolute. If the escape was due to a natural event the 'act of God' defence applies, as in **Nichols v Marsland 1876**. A second defence that applies to these two torts is act of a stranger. This applies where the nuisance or escape from D's land was someone else's fault, as in **Perry v Kendricks 1956**.

The contributory negligence defence recognises that D may not have been solely at fault, so that damages are reduced to reflect the amount that C is also blameworthy, as in **Gannon v Rotherham MBC 1991**. In **Belka v Prosperini 2011**, C had run across a dual carriageway near a roundabout having drunk about four pints of beer. He was hit by a taxi and claimed in negligence. The judge found that he was two-thirds to blame and reduced his damages accordingly under the **Law Reform (Contributory Negligence) Act**. He appealed, arguing that even if blame was to be shared he was not more blameworthy than D. The CA held that his was the greater fault because, although D had been negligent in not anticipating the risk of hitting someone, C had taken a deliberate risk by running across the road in front of the vehicle.

Any cases on contributory negligence and consent can be used to illustrate fault. In the first, damages are reduced according to the level of fault of C. In the second, C's level of fault is high enough to indicate implied consent to the resulting harm. These two defences therefore overlap. If the risk is obvious it may mean there is a full defence rather than a reduction in damages. In **Ratcliff v McConnell 1999**, a 19-year-old student was seriously injured diving into a swimming pool at his college. He had been drinking but the evidence was that he knew what he was doing. The court found that the risk of hitting his head on the bottom was obvious so the defence of consent succeeded.

As any reduction in damages (contributory negligence) or lack of liability (consent) is usually based on blameworthiness the defences are less likely to apply in the case of a child. The courts recognise that a child is less likely to see the risk of harm, as in **Yachuk v Oliver Blais 1949**. However, in **Jackson v Murray 2015**, the child was found to be 70% to blame and although the SC felt that a fairer apportionment would be one-third and two-thirds it held that the role of an appellate court was not to substitute its judgment for that of a court below unless it was plainly wrong. This decision did not properly reflect the level of fault because the accident would not have happened at all if he had not been driving too fast. It therefore seems wrong to reduce her damages by 70% even though she was at fault in stepping out from behind the minibus. However, in most cases contributory negligence provides a fairer result than the all-or-nothing nature of the defence of consent.

Task 20

There are plenty of other cases on these defences. Choose one for each defence and explain how it relates to fault.

Remedies are intended to compensate C rather than punish D, so do not necessarily reflect the degree of fault, just the amount of damage or harm done. However, D is only liable to pay compensation for *foreseeable* damage, as **The Wagon Mound** applies to remedies too, so fault is relevant at this last stage in proving liability. The more foreseeable something is, the more at fault you are for not avoiding it, so it seems fair that you are liable for the foreseeable consequences of your actions.

4.6 Liability without fault in civil law

We'll look at some examples of 'no-fault' liability in contract and tort, and then consider how far liability without fault *should* be imposed.

Contract

The rules on revocation and acceptance mean a contract can be formed unknowingly and so can be breached without any fault. In particular, the postal rule can be discussed. Acceptance by post is complete as soon as something is posted even if it doesn't arrive, as confirmed in **Household Insurance v Grant 1879**. This means the other party may not know that an offer has not been accepted. The **E-Commerce Directive 2002** does not change this as although it covers electronic contracts, it is the buyer who makes the offer which can then be accepted by the seller.

Example

Geoff offers to sell his car to Paul. Paul writes to accept but Geoff doesn't get the letter. Thinking Paul doesn't want the car, Geoff sells it to someone else. Paul can sue for breach of contract, but it can hardly be said that Geoff is at fault. The argument for this rule is that Geoff could exclude it by saying that acceptance must be in a particular form, or must reach him.

Many implied terms impose liability without fault. Thus, in **Godley v Perry 1960**, the seller could be sued for the catapult not being of satisfactory quality, even though not personally at fault. On the other hand, this will not apply if the defects were brought to the buyer's attention, or the goods were examined and the defect should have been noticed. This recognises that if C is at fault D should not be liable. In **Wilson v Best Travel 1993**, C fell through a glass door while on holiday. The tour operator had not breached the implied term under **s 13** of the **Sale of Goods and Services Act** – that the service would be carried out with reasonable care and skill – as they had checked the premises and there was no obvious danger, they were not at fault.

Innominate terms look at the effect of the breach on C, rather than the degree of fault by D. This means that whatever the level of fault, if the consequences are serious C can rescind the contract as well as claim damages.

Tort

One area of tort that has liability without fault is the **Consumer Protection Act 1987** (**CPA**) (now the **Consumer Rights Act 2015**). This Act imposed strict liability on producers, unlike the common law from **Donoghue v Stevenson 1932** where fault had to be proved. If a product has a defect and causes harm, the producer is liable without the need to prove negligence. This means that Mrs Donoghue would be able to sue the manufacturer of the ginger beer without having to prove any fault. Stevenson would be liable even if the bottles were properly checked for snails! A producer includes a manufacturer and others in similar positions. There are certain defences which allow some leeway, but the fact remains that a producer or manufacturer can be liable without fault.

The main area of strict liability in tort is **Rylands v Fletcher 1868**. There is no need to prove fault, i.e., C need not prove negligence, merely that something has escaped and caused damage. As Lord Cranworth said in the case itself, *"he is responsible, however careful he may have been, and whatever precautions he may have taken"*. This can be compared to negligence, which requires proof of breach of duty, and nuisance which has a lower level of fault than negligence but still requires unreasonableness. On the other hand, there are so many defences to this tort that it is often hard to prove liability at all. In addition, a small degree of fault has entered the law under **Rylands**, as D is only liable for foreseeable damage. Liability is strict in that if damage *is* foreseeable then D is liable regardless of the amount of care taken, but in **Cambridge Water Co 1994** the HL added that as with negligence if the damage is *not* foreseeable D will avoid liability.

The other area of tort where a person can be liable without fault is vicarious liability. As seen in the quote opening this chapter, it is not necessary to prove an employer is at fault in any way. In fact, if the employer *is* at fault there will be primary, rather than vicarious liability. Fault is still an important element, as C must prove the negligence (breach) by the employee. However, it is the employer who is sued, and who will pay any compensation, not the person actually at fault.

Example

Julie is stacking shelves in Tesco and drops a bottle of oil. She leaves the spillage and goes for her tea break and a woman shopper slips and is injured. The customer can sue Tesco on the basis of vicarious liability for Julie's negligence. Tesco can be both vicariously for Julie's actions, and primarily liable, e.g., for having poorly trained staff. In both cases the customer will sue Tesco, but in the first, she must prove Julie was negligent, in the second that Tesco was.

Vicarious liability applies even to acts which seem well outside the scope of employment, such as sexual activities, as seen in **Lister v Helsey Hall 2001**. It may seem wrong that an employer can be liable even though not at fault, but the law needs to protect the victim and an employer is not only more likely to be able to pay, but also is able to insure against such claims. In **Mohamud v WM Morrison Supermarkets plc 2016**, the SC considered **Lister** and applied the close connection test. C had been assaulted by a petrol attendant following some verbal abuse and the CA had held that his work was to serve and help customers so the assault was outside the scope of his employment. The SC reversed the decision and held that although D may have abused his position his actions still came within the scope of his employment. The SC made clear there were two questions. The first was what the nature of the job was, and this should be addressed broadly. The second involved whether there was sufficient connection between that job and the wrongful conduct to make it right for the employer to be held liable under the principle of social justice. There seems less justification for imposing vicarious liability in non-employment situations. However, vicarious liability was imposed on a local council for abuse by foster parents in **Armes 2017**. The CA had found the council not liable but the SC allowed the appeal and held that the council had sufficient control over the choice of foster parents, and a supervisory role in respect of holidays and medical treatment, and this justified imposing liability. Lord Hughes dissented saying *"Vicarious liability is strict liability, imposed on a party who has been in no sense at fault"* adding that it was fair and proper in employment and other commercial cases but extending it *"needs careful justification"*. It can be argued that his is the preferred view and the courts have gone too far in imposing liability without fault in situations like these.

4.7 Whether there should be liability without fault in civil law

So why do the courts impose liability on someone who appears blameless? There is not a great deal of controversy in contract law on this issue. Since the courts created the doctrine of frustration in **Taylor v Caldwell 1863**, there is no longer liability for breach of a contract which has become impossible to perform. Until then it was unfair that people could be sued for breach through no fault of their own. Possibly the rules on offer and acceptance are still unfair, as the offeror may not know an offer has been accepted if the postal rule applies. There is an argument that in a world of instant communication the rule should be abolished so a person cannot unknowingly, and without fault, breach a contract.

As regards tort and how far fault should a requirement, this has been much debated over the years. The question was the subject of the **Pearson Commission Report** in 1978, and this is a good base for a discussion of the idea of fault-based liability as opposed to strict liability.

4.8 The Pearson Commission Report and calls for reform

The Commission was set up because it was recognised that there are many problems for people who have suffered damage or harm. Fault can be hard to prove and many victims are left without compensation for their injuries. One of the main arguments for the introduction of a no-fault compensation scheme is that the tort system is too irrational in providing different levels of remedy for the same type of accident, and sometimes no remedy at all.

The Commission felt the tort system, for all its faults, should be retained, but supplemented by a more widespread system of social security, e.g., a no-fault compensation scheme was suggested whereby road accident victims could be compensated from a fund administered by the state and funded by about a penny on a gallon of petrol. Tort would remain as an alternative. The Commission also recommended a no-fault scheme for product liability, ultra-hazardous activities and authorised vaccines. The first is now covered by the **Consumer Protection Act** and the last by the **Vaccine Damage Act**, but the recommendation that strict liability should be imposed on 'ultra hazardous' activities was not implemented – although there are one or two Acts dealing with particular areas such as oil pollution and nuclear installations. Such activities are partly covered by the rule in **Rylands v Fletcher,** but many would prefer them to be governed by statute, as **Rylands** is seen as unpredictable. In **Cambridge Water** and **Transco 2004**, the HL, although declining to abolish the rule, also declined to extend the scope of strict liability further, indicating that it was for Parliament to legislate. Legislation would be able properly to regulate dangerous activities and provide that insurance is compulsory for people dealing in dangerous materials or 'ultra-hazardous' activities.

There was some expectation that a no-fault scheme for medical accidents would be put forward but only a further investigation of the no-fault system then operating in New Zealand was suggested. This applied to all accident victims and was funded by vehicle licences, levies on employers and taxes. It was abandoned in 1991 when the economy went into recession. In the UK nothing further was done and the problems continued to be the subject of much debate. The **NHS Redress Act 2006** was supposed to help. When introducing the legislation the government recognised that medical negligence claims were lengthy, slow and costly, with legal fees often exceeding the claim. They were also seen as unfair, with too many variations in outcome (as the Pearson Committee noted). The **Act** would have allowed for compensation up to £20,000 to be paid without the need for a court action, although with the right to sue still available. The government made clear that fault-based liability should remain the norm for compensation claims but the scheme was intended to offer an alternative to litigation. The emphasis was on getting it right rather than apportioning blame and the scheme was meant to help to speed up the process of getting compensation and to avoid the stress of going to court. The Act has not been brought into effect so the system is still fault-based. Medical negligence claims continue to clog up the courts and eat up NHS resources. One of the reasons for not implementing the **NHS Redress Act** was that changes to legal aid were imminent. However, these have not helped; in fact individuals who have suffered injury are worse off. Since the changes introduced by **LASPO** in April 2013, the solicitor's success fee is no longer payable by the losing side. This means the winning party must pay the extra, thus reducing the amount of damages recovered. This can be up to 100% of the normal fee, although it must not exceed 25% of the damages in personal injury cases. A no-fault compensation scheme of some sort may have alleviated the problems; **LASPO** has exacerbated them.

Arguments for a no-fault system

- ***The benefits and burdens are distributed more evenly so that compensation comes from a group of people not one individual, e.g., by motorists through car insurance***
- ***Everyone is compensated, though possibly to a lesser degree***
- ***It makes people take care to ensure people and premises are safe***
- ***The benefit to society of many hazardous activities (e.g., in industry or medicine) means society not the individual business should bear the burden of paying compensation***
- ***It limits the number of court cases, so courts are not overloaded***
- ***The fault system can be unfair as sometimes C is fully compensated but sometimes gets nothing***
- ***Proving fault is time-consuming and costly and a no-fault system would be cheaper to operate***
- ***The adversarial nature of court proceedings means it may make a relationship worse, e.g., in employment cases or in nuisance cases between neighbours***

Arguments for a fault system

- ***The wrongdoer pays***
- ***A no-fault system would be a move away from individual responsibility***
- ***If fault is proved C is fully compensated***
- ***A no-fault system may not make D more careful***
- ***The conditional fee scheme – 'no win, no fee' – helps C to claim without the worry of solicitor's fees***
- ***Changes to this scheme in April 2013 do not affect making a claim, as they only apply after a case is won. However, now C has to pay the success fee from any award of compensation***

Task 21

You will need to develop these arguments so pick a few that make sense and expand on them. If possible use a case to illustrate. Keep your notes for later revision.

Examination tip

Whatever topics you are using to illustrate your answer, be sure to relate your cases to the specific question. You will need to do more than explain fault and/or strict liability. Read the question carefully to see what you should focus on, e.g., you may be asked to discuss how *important* fault is in proving liability or whether fault *should* be proved before someone can be liable. Use cases you are comfortable explaining to support what you say; perhaps including some where you feel the outcome was unjust because D had a low level of fault.

summary

Note the importance of fault in proving liability and the cases where no fault is required

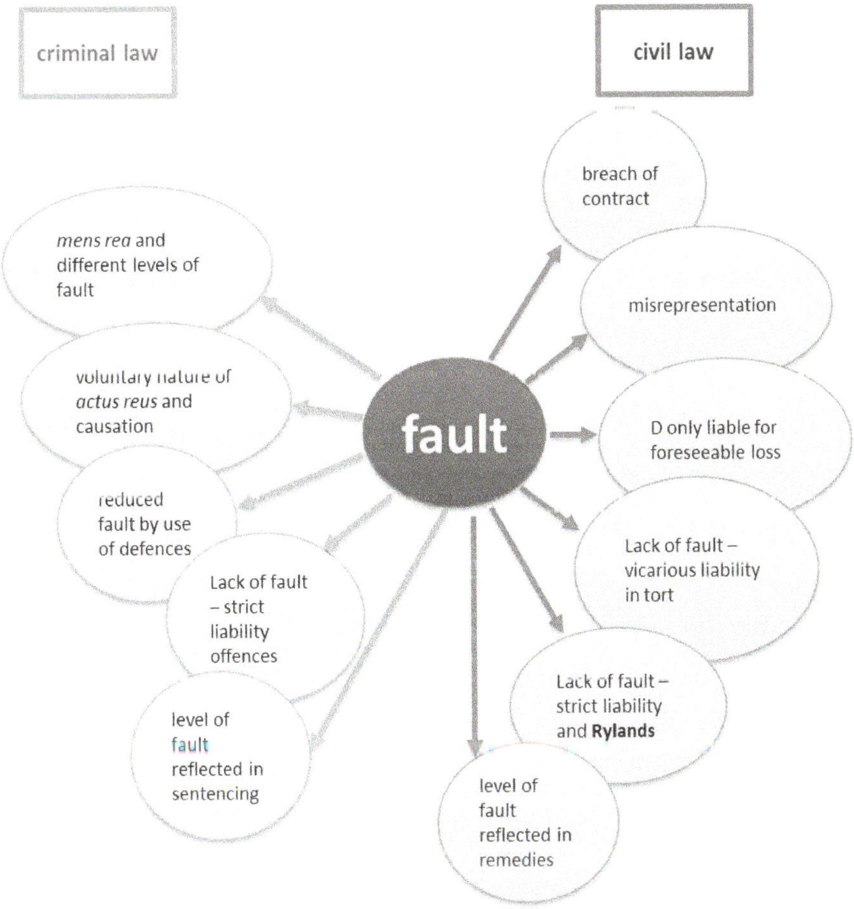

Self-test questions

1. *Explain how fault is proved in either civil or criminal law*
2. *How may a defence reflect the degree of fault involved?*
3. *Explain two cases where there was no liability because fault could not be proved*
4. *Use two cases to support an argument for imposing/not imposing strict liability*
5. *How did **Cambridge Water** add a degree of fault to the strict liability rule under **Rylands?***

For answers to the tasks and self-test questions, please go to my website at www.drsr.org and click the button 'Answers to Kindle tasks'

> *"There is a contest here between the interest of the public at large and the interest of a private individual"*

Lord Denning MR in ***Miller v Jackson 1977***

By the end of this Chapter you should be able to:

- ***Identify the competing interests in society***
- ***Explain how the law attempts to achieve a fair balance between such interests***
- ***Use cases and examples to show how the law is used to 'engineer' this balance***

Before we consider how interests might conflict we first need to understand what an interest is.

5.1 Public and private interests

Interests conflict in all areas of public and private life – from drafting anti-terrorism legislation to deciding which TV programmes to watch. The law cannot satisfy all interests, so will attempt to satisfy as many as possible. This will usually be the dominant group in a society. There is a need to balance individual interests against each other, and also against those of society. Private interests may be subordinated to those of the community – the utilitarian theory of maximising happiness can be seen in this.

Example

Westminster County Council plans to regulate the use of delivery apps by spring 2018. This is because residents have complained that the mopeds congregating on street corners while waiting for an order are a nuisance. Restaurants who make a lot of deliveries will need to apply for special planning permission. This is an example of balancing the private interest in getting food delivered with the public interest in a quiet environment. The private interest is subordinate so the law will restrict the activity in the public interest. However, a balance is achieved by regulating the behaviour rather than banning it.

When looking at the legal process, cases and legislation consider the following questions:

- **What are the interests that might conflict here?**
- **What is an appropriate balance between those interests?**
- **Has this particular case/Act/process achieved that balance?**
- ***How* has the law 'engineered' the balance?**

Examination tip

There is a clear overlap with justice. Theories of justice attempt to *define* justice. Balancing competing interests is an attempt to *achieve* justice. You can therefore mention one or two theories from Law and Justice. A *utilitarian*, like Bentham, might say justice is best achieved by balancing the interests to ensure the greatest good for the greatest number. A *libertarian* like Mill would want any balance to take into account individual autonomy, or freedom of choice, so the law should only interfere in this freedom where harm may be caused to others. A *Marxist* would want to ensure that individuals receive what they need whilst contributing what they can. Aristotle would suggest redistribution in proportion to people's claims to benefits to balance the interests. As an *egalitarian,*

Rawls would want any redistribution to be equal. Nozick would claim that any state-initiated redistribution was unjust.

Task 22

Remind yourself of Aristotle's theory of distributive justice in the Chapter on Law and Justice. How could you use this theory to support the decision of the court in **Miller v Jackson 1977** not to award an injunction?

Bentham saw the role of the law as balancing interests to achieve maximum happiness, 'the greatest good'. He influenced the work of **Jhering (1818 – 1892)**. Jhering, another utilitarian, emphasised the needs of society when balancing interests. He saw law as a form of social engineering, ordering the way society behaved. Whether the law was just was measured by how far it achieved a proper balance in resolving the conflict in society between people's social interests and people's individual interests. Jhering's work was in turn relied on by one of the key writers on the subject of competing interests – the American academic lawyer, Roscoe **Pound**.

Roscoe Pound

Pound (1870 – 1964) regarded law as an engineering tool, a form of social control. He studied law's position in society and how it could be used to 'engineer' a balance between the different interests within society. He developed the theory of social engineering building on the theories of Bentham and Jhering. Where interests are in conflict, the law should try to engineer a balance which will achieve social cohesion. The purpose of law is to satisfy as many interests as possible. The maximum number of wants satisfied with the minimum amount of friction and waste. Where interests conflicted, they had to be weighed, or balanced, against each other with the aim of satisfying as many as possible. Pound developed Jhering's theory of using the law to achieve a balance, but argued that interests could only be balanced on the same level. Thus, social interests should not be balanced against individual interests, only other social interests, and *vice versa*. An example would be the debate on smoking in public. In Pound's view, the individual interests of those who want a ban (avoiding passive smoking) can be balanced against the interests of those who don't (freedom of choice), as they are on the same level, but not against the wider social interests. Alternatively, the social benefits (lots of tax on cigarettes which helps pay for other social benefits) and burdens (health problems, burden on the NHS) can be balanced against each other, but these shouldn't be balanced against the individual's interests.

Neither Parliament nor the courts has always followed Pound's theory in so far as balancing interests only on the same level is concerned. Both social and individual interests were taken into account during the debates which preceded the smoking ban. However, we can see how the law is being used to 'engineer' the way society behaves – to stop people smoking.

The idea of the law acting to resolve conflict, and 'engineering' a balance between competing interests, is seen in many areas.

Examination tip

You need to make sure you address the question if asked to focus on a particular area and there are plenty of examples in this chapter. However, examiners like to see independent thought and new ideas. You can therefore add some topical issues to an essay. The law is involved in many more areas than you might realise, and the media carry stories every day that can be used to illustrate a discussion of balancing interests. It is unlikely that people will agree on issues like fox hunting, smoking and whether a school can tell the children what to eat or what not to watch on TV, so there will always be a lot of debate when the law gets involved in such areas.

5.2 Interests: claim rights and residual freedoms

An interest is similar to a right. With most rights come corresponding duties. Thus in criminal and civil law we have a right not to be harmed. This imposes a corresponding duty on others not to cause harm, whether in criminal law or through negligence. In contract law we have a right to receive goods and a duty to pay the agreed price. The other party to the contract has a corresponding duty to supply the goods and a right to receive payment. In legal procedure there is a right to legal advice following an arrest and a corresponding duty to provide access to a solicitor. This correspondence principle was put forward by an American law professor, Wesley **Hohfeld** (1879 – 1918). He also noted that people, including lawyers, used the word 'right' rather indiscriminately and attempted to clarify it by comparing rights to liberties (or freedoms). A right can be claimed and comes with a corresponding duty, as in the right to the contract price (Hohfeld referred to this as a claim right). A liberty is the freedom to do as you choose and this imposes no corresponding duty (this is a privilege not a right that can be claimed). We saw in Chapters 2 and 3 that Mill was a libertarian, so felt people should be free to choose how to act as long as it did not harm others. Only then should the law step in. His theory would prefer interests to be liberties rather than rights. That would give greater freedom of choice as it would not impose duties (other than the duty not to harm others). Rights can be claimed, liberties cannot.

Example

I have a right not to be harmed by someone's negligence and can claim that right. I can ask the law to enforce it by making a claim in court. I have a liberty to go to a pop concert, but I cannot claim it as a right if the concert is sold out and I can't get in. However, if I had a ticket this would give me a contractual right so I could claim this right and sue for breach of contract.

Some countries, such as America and Germany, have a constitution which gives rights. These are claim rights and are enforceable by law. Other countries, like the UK, have a system based on freedoms. The UK system means anything not specifically prohibited is allowed, but is not enforceable by law. So there are claim rights and residual freedoms, or liberties.

Example

There is a sign in the park saying 'no cycling'. This is a rule (probably a council by-law) and if it is disobeyed the rule can be enforced by law, usually by imposing a fine.

There is no sign in the park. In Germany, this means you cannot cycle as there is no notice permitting it. In the UK, it means you can cycle; it is not forbidden so you are free to do it. This is a residual freedom, what is left after the law has regulated what you must or must not do. You cannot however, claim that you have a right to cycle.

There is a sign in the park saying 'cycling is permitted'. This would be a claim right and enforceable by law. If someone tries to stop you cycling you can say *"I have a right to cycle here"*.

UK citizens have some rights but these mostly come from international law e.g., the rights from the **European Convention on Human Rights (ECHR)** which are part of UK law by way of the **Human Rights Act 1998 (HRA)**. Other rights come under **The Charter of Fundamental Rights of the European Union**, at least for now.

Rights and freedoms (interests) often compete. I have a right to free speech but this is constrained by a person's right not to be defamed by untrue statements and by the right to privacy. My right to free speech also allows me to protest against unjust laws. If lots of people protest there may be a danger of disrupting public order. This is where the rights and freedoms may need balancing. In the first example the law must balance freedom of speech against the right not to be defamed. In the second it must balance the need for free speech in a democratic society against the need to maintain order to protect that society.

So the law protects people's rights by imposing a duty on others not to interfere with those rights. Whether making or enforcing the law, Parliament and the courts must balance people's rights and freedoms and try to satisfy as many interests as possible. Whether civil or criminal, all cases involve some kind of balancing process between the interests of the parties involved. Many cases also involve the wider public interest and the law will take this into account as well.

The tools

The 'engineering tools' used to try and balance the interests are:

- **the substantive law**
- **the legal process**
- **sanctions and remedies**

As you look at the examples in each of these, ask yourself the four questions under 'public and private interests' above.

5.3 The substantive law

Whichever area of law you are studying, you'll find plenty of cases to choose from. Here are a few ideas. I have not included the full facts as you should know these from your study of the topic. However, the most recent cases may not be in every text book so I have added more on these. The cases and examples are based on my books (check my website at www.drsr.org or look on Amazon for what's available if you are interested in buying one).

Examination tip

Before looking at case examples it is worth noting how to use them. First choose a case that you understand and identify the interests that are involved. Then look at how they compete and how the law has engineered a balance between them. Finally, consider whether justice has been achieved and for whom. You can use your own opinion on this but where possible you should also refer to a theory of justice. Here is an example.

Example

In **Brown 1994** the interests of the individuals conflicted with the public interest and the law favoured the public interest (as Pound predicted would happen when public and private interests conflict). Whether justice was achieved depends on your opinion and on the theory of justice. Natural law would say justice was achieved for society as a whole as the decision was based on morality. A utilitarian would probably see justice as achieved because the protection of society prevailed over personal autonomy. This would satisfy the most interests and thus maximise happiness. A libertarian like Mill would say justice was not achieved for the individuals concerned as they were not allowed freedom of choice. You could usefully choose a second case to compare where the facts are similar but the balance achieved a different outcome. In **Wilson 1996**, there was also consensual serious harm but this was between a man and his wife. This time when balancing the interests, the law favoured the freedom of the individual. A utilitarian would probably have said justice was achieved as society did not need protecting, as would Mill who favoured freedom of choice. Natural law might still regard the behaviour as immoral and expect the law to intervene to protect society.

This chapter will identify how competing interests are weighed up and balanced during the making and application of the law and illustrate this by using cases from the various areas of substantive and procedural law which you study.

Crime

The public interest is taken into account when making and applying the law. The right not to be harmed is balanced against the concept of personal autonomy, but the courts will also look at the wider impact on society as seen in **Brown 1994**. As with law and morals and law and justice, the right to life is also balanced against personal autonomy. This takes into account the public interest in the sanctity of life and can be illustrated by the murder, manslaughter and euthanasia cases discussed in Chapter 2 and Chapter 3. Another case which illustrates this conflict is **Re E 2012**. In that case the court ordered that an anorexic girl should be force fed against her wishes. As with euthanasia, when balancing the competing interests the court decided that the sanctity of life prevailed over freedom of choice. Although not strictly a criminal case, it could have become one if force-feeding had been done without a court order as it would have been at least a battery, if not a more serious offence. This is similar to **Bland 1993** where, without the court declaration, it could have been murder.

Pound recognised that where public and private interests were in conflict the public interest would prevail. This was seen in **Brown** discussed above. It is also illustrated by strict liability offences. Strict liability crimes clearly favour the public interest and subordinate the individual interest to the public interest in being protected as in **Meah v Roberts 1977** and **Harrow LBC v Shah 1999**. Environmental laws which make matters such as pollution strict liability offences also favour the public interest, as in **Alphacell**. The public interest in conflict with the private can also be seen in relation to defences. Society has a right not to allow criminals to cause harm, steal or commit other offences. Individuals within society have the same rights. These rights are balanced against the interests of D in having a defence to the crime. With duress the law balances the interest of the public in being protected against those of D, who has only committed the crime due to a threat of serious harm. In this case, if the defence succeeds, the private interest prevails. In cases of murder it does not apply because the public interest in the sanctity of life prevails, as in **Wilson 2007**. All defences illustrate an attempt by the law to achieve a fair balance between public and private interests.

The role of the law is to protect property as well as people, so a person who has taken something from another should be punished. However, a balance may need to be considered where there is a reason for the theft. **S 2** of the **Theft Act** addresses this by providing for three situations where D will not be found dishonest and so will not be guilty of theft even though appropriating another's property. This tips the balance in D's favour where there is an honest belief that the property could be taken for one of the three reasons.

Here are a few more examples.

Bratty v A-G for Northern Ireland 1963	• Lord Denning said a disorder which led to violence and was prone to recur was "the sort of disease for which a person should be retained in hospital rather than be given an unqualified acquittal." The law on insanity can be used to protect society.
O' Grady 1987	•"There are two competing interests. On the one hand the interest of D who has only acted according to what he believed to be necessary to protect himself, and on the other hand that of the public in general, and the victim in particular who, probably through no fault of his own, has been injured or perhaps killed because of D's drunken mistake." CA
Brown 1994	• The Lords' decision was partly based on the need to protect society from what was seen as deviant behaviour. This outweighed the rights of the individuals to personal autonomy. Lord Templeman said society was entitled to protect itself against a cult of violence.
Wilson 1996	• Society did not need protecting so the balance tipped in favour of D.
Hasan 2005	• The law must balance the public interest in being safe against the interests of D who was forced to act. The HL decided that there must be no alternative action available to D.

Task 23

Choose a case from crime, or use one of my examples. Write a brief note of the facts and the judgement. Identify the interests which competed and then add a little on how, and whether, you think that the court achieved an appropriate balance between these competing interests, using a theory if possible.

Contract

Contract law is based on the idea of agreement. In general, the courts are reluctant to interfere in order to engineer a balance of interests, preferring to allow the parties freedom to contract as they wish. However, there are times when a person's interests may need protecting, particularly where one party is in a weaker position than the other. The law attempts to redress the imbalance by making laws protecting the weaker party such as the **Consumer Rights Act 2015**.

Here are a few examples of competing interests in contract law.

The Moorcock 1889	• The court may impose terms into a contract to engineer a just balance and ensure 'business efficacy'.
Oscar Chess Ltd v Willams1957	• A statement by a seller as to a car's age was held to be a representation, not a term. Compare this to **Dick Bentley Productions v Harold Smith Motors Ltd 1965**, where a statement that a car had only done 20,000 miles was held to be a term. The non-expert needs greater protection than the specialist.
Consumer Rights Act 2015	• This consolidates other consumer protection laws and attempts to achieve a just balance by giving protection to a consumer when dealing with a business, which is in a more powerful position.
Williams v Roffey 1990	• The court was prepared to weigh up the various interests in finding consideration. The act of finishing the work was enough to enforce the offer of extra payment, even though this was no more than had been agreed. It was a just balance based on the reality of the situation.
Wessanen Foods Ltd v Jofson Ltd 2006	• The court felt that in relation to a business agreement where the parties had equality of bargaining power an exclusion clause was reasonable. This achieves a balance between protection and non-interference. The courts are less likely to interfere in a contract where the parties deal on equal terms.

Tort

Tort provides plenty of examples. When it was established that a manufacturer could owe a duty of care to a consumer the HL in **Donoghue v Stevenson 1932** balanced the interests of the victim of harm to be compensated with the interests of the manufacturer in not being liable to anyone and everyone. The HL established that there could be liability to people without a contract but it was limited to having a duty to avoid foreseeable harm and the duty was only owed to those within D's contemplation when acting. In **Caparo** this was developed, so that now when proving a duty of care in negligence the courts will ask whether it is fair, just and reasonable to impose a duty on policy grounds. This involves balancing the right of C to compensation not only against the cost to D, but also against the wider community interests. This is particularly evident in cases involving the police, rescue services, hospitals and schools where compensation would usually come from public funds (i.e., tax-payers). The private interest must be balanced against the cost to society both in financial terms and in efficiency. As Pound made clear, private interests will be subordinate to public interests and the law has a difficult task when it comes to accidents involving emergency services. The balancing of competing public and private interests can be seen in both duty and breach where the courts will take into account policy issues. In **Hill v CC of West Yorkshire 1988**, there was no duty owed by the police for policy reasons. It was not in the public interest because compensation would come from public funds and imposing a duty could make policing less effective. This is a just result as more people are protected by the police being effective, thus maximising happiness. However, in **Michael v CC of South Wales 2015**, the SC refused to find a duty owed by the police even though there had been direct contact. This time allowing the public interest to prevail did not achieve justice because the police knew of the threatened harm so should have acted to protect the victim. For other examples look at cases which were decided on the third part of the **Caparo** test. If you have my tort book, see the section headed 'Police, councils and sporting bodies'.

Policy comes into breach because one factor the courts take into account is whether there is any social benefit. In **Watts v Herts CC 1954**, there was no breach by the fire service because it was an emergency. It is not in the public interest to find a breach of duty in such circumstances. As with **Hill v CC of West Yorkshire 1988** on duty, it could lead to a less efficient service. However, the courts have made clear that the emergency services are not immune from liability and must take reasonable care. In **MacLeod v MPC 2015**, a police car driving at speed (but with the siren going and the blue light flashing) collided with a cyclist. Both the above policy arguments arose. However, despite the fact that compensation would come from public funds and imposing liability might make the public services too cautious when responding to an emergency, the court found both duty and breach. The driver had not taken sufficient care and was liable in negligence. The CA upheld the decision. The case shows that although the public interest may trump the private interest, this is not an absolute. **Vernon Knight Associates v Cornwall CC 2013** is another example where the private interest prevailed over the public interest (in proving both duty and breach). Here the council knew of the drainage problem but did not act. Arguably this is like **Michael v CC of South Wales 2015** so supports the argument that a duty should have been imposed on the police in those circumstances.

Other than policy reasons, there are other factors which are balanced against each other when proving breach of duty. As well as any benefit to society, the courts will look at how foreseeable/high the risk is, whether the victim is vulnerable and so can expect greater care, and whether it is reasonable to expect D to take further precautions. The interests of both C and D are weighed in the balance by this process. In addition, the **Compensation Act 2006** attempts to protect people from being sued when they are undertaking a 'desirable activity', such as school trips and sports. This takes into account the public interest in having such activities.

A particularly good area to explore competing interests is the tort of nuisance. In **Hunter v Canary Wharf 1997**, the HL said nuisance involved *"striking a balance between the interests of neighbours"*. I have not included case examples here because you don't need to pick and choose, *all* nuisance cases illustrate an attempt to balance competing interests. One person's freedom can be another's misery.

Example

I work late in a nightclub and when I get home I want to relax and enjoy some music. This is fine if I live in a detached house miles from anyone, but I live in a terrace with neighbours on either side. My right to play music at 3 a.m. has to be balanced against the neighbour's right to a good night's sleep.

Another area to consider is defences. The **Law Reform (Contributory Negligence) Act 1945** is an example of balancing interests to achieve a fairer result. This is done by taking into account the fact that C is partly to blame. Again, any cases on this defence can be used to illustrate the attempt of the law to balance competing interests.

Examination tip

A good way to illustrate the defence of contributory negligence in regard to the balance is to choose two cases and contrast them. **Jackson v Murray 2015** can be used to show the courts do not always achieve a just balance because the case involved a child and the driver had been going too fast. The reduction in damages by 70% was too high. This can be compared to **Taylor v English Heritage 2016** where a fairer balance was achieved. A 50% reduction more accurately reflected the amount of fault of both parties because English Heritage should have put up a sign but the man did not take any precautions to avoid the harm.

Remedies are aimed at balancing the private interests of the parties to the action (as in all nuisance cases) but also involve the public interest, especially when an injunction is sought. The courts will need to balance all these interests to decide on whether to grant an injunction. A clear example is **Miller v Jackson 1977** where the public interest in having cricket prevailed over Mrs Miller's private interest so the court refused the injunction. As Pound noted, where public and private interests conflict and are put in the balance the result is likely to favour the public interest. At one time it was said that an injunction should be the normal remedy in a nuisance case. This was confirmed in **Regan v Paul Properties Ltd 2006** where C had complained about D's building blocking his light. The court held that it would be wrong not to issue an injunction because damages would not help and would effectively allow D to buy a right to cause a nuisance. However, this principle is no longer dominant. In **Lawrence v Fen Tigers Ltd (No 2) 2014**, the SC suggested that the principle of relying on an injunction as the normal remedy was out of date. Lord Neuberger said "*it is unfortunate that it has been followed so recently and so slavishly*" and noted that it had been devised at a time when there was less property and fewer statutory controls. When balancing competing interests, especially when the public interest lies in refusing an injunction, the courts may more readily award compensation instead, as was the case in **Miller v Jackson**.

The following are just a few cases from tort to illustrate competing interests.

Christie v Davey 1893

- balancing the right of one neighbour to give piano lessons against the other's right to quiet enjoyment of their property

Latimer v AEC 1952

- the right of an individual to compensation is subordinated to the wider community interest of keeping the factory open

Watts v Herts CC 1954

- balancing the right of an individual to compensation against the fact that it was a rescue operation. As it was the Fire Service any compensation would come from public funds

Miller v Jackson 1977

- private interests (C's right to quiet enjoyment) were again subordinated to community interests (the playing of cricket)

Harris v Perry 2008

- a balance has to be struck between the interests of children being able to play, and the interests of the community as a whole in being protected from harm

Task 24

Choose a case on contract or tort, or use one of my examples. Identify the interests then add a little on how, and whether, you think that the court achieved an appropriate balance between them, using a theory if possible.

Human rights

There are wide-ranging rights under the **European Convention on Human Rights (ECHR)** and many cases have been heard both in the UK domestic courts and in the ECtHR in Strasbourg. This area is important when balancing competing interests, especially **A 8** and **A 10** cases as these articles are in conflict not only with other public or private interests but also with each other. Here are a few examples, where the freedoms under the **ECHR** were in conflict either with other freedoms or with the public interest (public health or state security). As all human rights cases involve competing interests of some sort, rather than using a table I have given a bit more detail in the case examples.

The right to life under Article 2 ECHR: 'Designer' babies and euthanasia

Interests were in conflict in **Quintavalle v Human Fertilisation and Embryology Authority 2005** (see law and morals). The HL had to try to find a balance between the private interests of those involved and the wider interests of the public, those who believed in the sanctity of life and those who were 'pro-choice'. While recognising the case raised *"profound ethical questions"*, the HL held that the Act allowed tissue typing, but in limited circumstances. Individual autonomy (Mill) prevailed over natural law (Aristotle and Aquinas).

There is a clear overlap with morals and justice. Any of the cases on euthanasia and assisted suicide involve balancing the right to life against personal autonomy. Look back at the chapters on morals and justice for more on these and other issues where there were competing interests. However, you will need to change the emphasis to one involving the competing interests rather than the issue of morals, so concentrate on considering whose interests the court was trying to protect and whether the balance was successful. Controversial cases like this are useful in illustrating not only how the courts are required to balance competing interests, but also in illustrating the difficulties in doing so.

Example

In assisted suicide cases, there are privates interests in conflict and there is also a conflict between the private and public interests. The private interests are the right to choose the time and manner of your own death against the right to be protected from those who might encourage a suicide because you have become a burden. The public interest lies in the argument that taking a life for any reason weakens society as a whole. Law is a tool for engineering a fair balance between competing interests. However, until Parliament acts, judges must balance these interests to protect the majority and base legal decisions on what is best for society. The individual in the case may feel that justice has not been achieved in this balancing act but, as a utilitarian would argue, the law should aim to maximise the greatest overall benefit.

Where opinion on a subject is so divided it is almost impossible to satisfy the interests of any particular group, and neither Parliament nor the courts can be said to be wholly successful in resolving the conflicts. Law is sometimes an imperfect tool but it is arguably the best one for balancing interests against each other, as it is more likely to be impartial when reaching any decision.

The competing freedoms under the **ECHR** have to be balanced against each other as well as against other interests. The **Human Rights Act 1998 (HRA)** brings the rights into UK law but a judge cannot set aside a law that conflicts with them, only issue a declaration that the law is not compatible. However, the effect is much the same as once such a declaration is made the law is usually amended accordingly.

The right to respect for a private and family life and freedom of expression: Article 8 and **Article 10 ECHR**

A 8 is very wide-ranging and would cover several issues we have looked at before. The right to die and withdrawal of treatment can come under **A 2** or **A 8**. These and other **A 8** cases are covered with law and morals in Chapter 2. See the table at the end of this section for some examples.

A 8 also covers protection against intrusive media attention and this is in conflict with **A 10**. There have been many cases arguing the competing interests of freedom to a private life for public figures, and freedom of expression for the media and others who wish to write about those lives.

The following examples of the competing interests between privacy and freedom of speech include some where the balance favoured **A 8** and some where the balance favoured **A 10**. They are just a few from the many cases brought both in the ECtHR in Strasbourg and, since the **HRA** came into force in 2000, the UK courts.

In **Campbell v MGN 2004**, Naomi Campbell brought a case against MGN for publishing photographs of her leaving a Narcotics Anonymous meeting and suggesting she was a drug addict. The court held that her right to respect for private life under **Article 8 ECHR** outweighed MGN's right to freedom of expression under **Article 10**. The CA then reversed this decision and the case went to the HL. The HL upheld the original decision, but by a majority of only 3-2. This shows how difficult it is to achieve a fair balance. The importance of this case is the two-stage test it established. First the court must decide if there was an expectation of privacy. Second it must balance that expectation under **A 8** with the publisher's rights under **A 10**.

A case where the balance tipped the other way involved the footballer Rio Ferdinand against the same media company. In **Ferdinand v MGN Ltd 2011**, he tried to prevent publication of an article alleging that he had had an affair. In several articles and in his autobiography he had given the impression that he was a family man and had given up 'playing around'. He was also the England captain, so his conduct was of special interest to the public. The court held that the balance of interest lay in protecting the publisher's freedom of expression over the footballer's right to privacy.

In **Murray v Express Newspapers 2008**, JK Rowling brought a case on behalf of her young son following the publication of secretly taken photographs of him. Although the court made clear that the rights were equal, on the facts the child's rights under **A 8** trumped the publisher's rights under **A 10**. The two-stage test was approved and the balance tipped in favour of the privacy of the child. As a comparison, the balance tipped the other way in another case involving photographs of a child, **AAA v Associated Newspapers 2013**. In this case, although the interests of the child were taken into account, this time they carried less weight. Some information had already been published so it was a reduced expectation of privacy that had to be balanced against the public interest in being informed (a high-profile politician was allegedly the father of the child). The public interest prevailed. The two-stage test was approved again in **Weller 2015** and the court made clear that if the case involved a child the age was a relevant factor. Other factors included the nature and purpose of the intrusion. The court made clear that a child's rights to privacy did not trump **A 10** rights but *"they must be given considerable weight"*. The pictures were of a Paul Weller (former member of the Style Council) and his children. Although he was a public figure and the pictures were taken in a public place, it was a private family outing. This tipped the balance in favour of the private interests of the children under **A 8**.

In **V v Associated Newspapers and Others 2016**, the family's **A 8** rights were in conflict with the media's **A 10** rights in a 'right to die' case. The case attracted a lot of media attention as the woman was a well-known socialite, only aged 50 and not fatally ill. The Daily Mail referred to the *"socialite* *who chose death over growing old and ugly"*. The court allowed treatment to be withdrawn (balancing sanctity of life over personal autonomy, with the latter prevailing) but made a restriction order on press coverage to protect the family (balancing the public interest in the case with the family's right to respect for a private life). The press appealed but the order was upheld. The court recognised there was a public interest in cases like this, and also in having inquests open and public. However, the scales tipped towards protecting the private interests. A particular factor in the balance was that the youngest daughter had already shown signs of a fragile mental health and the court felt she would suffer further, especially at school, if her mother's identity was revealed. The restriction order was upheld.

In **Middleton 2016**, the court again suggested that there is no difference in the values of **A 8** and **A 10** and the circumstances of the case would always be relevant when deciding on the balance. In this case, Pippa Middleton's iCloud account had been illegally accessed and she sought a court order to prevent any photographs or other data being published prior to bringing a claim in court. In deciding whether or not to make the order the court looked at both sides of the arguments and at the circumstances. The court held that her arguments that her right under **A 8** would be infringed if the order was not made were *"very strong"*. In contrast, any argument that **A 10** would be infringed if the court order was made were said to be *"very weak"*.

These cases, along with the fact that there were so many appeals and reversals in **Douglas v Hello!** (in respect of unauthorised photographs of his wedding to Catherine Zeta Jones), highlight the difficulties of getting the balance right.

Another issue is technology. The digital age has increased the availability and accessibility of information. This is illustrated in **Middleton** above, and again in **PJS v NGN Ltd 2016**. Here the High Court granted an injunction to prevent the Sun publishing the name of an entertainer having extra-marital sex with another couple. The Sun had said *"The law is an ass"* because it meant that his right to cheat beat the rights of the Sun's readers to know about it. The CA allowed the appeal by the Sun, partly because it recognised the difficulty of keep secrets in a digital age. The case went to the SC. The SC ruled that the injunction should remain to give some protection to the children and said that even though the story may be of interest to members of the public, there was no public interest as such in 'kiss and tell' stories. The public interest element was minimal so his **A 8** rights should prevail. The difficulty of enforcing injunctions in a digital age should not mean that no injunction should be granted. The information may be 'out there' but it has to be searched for. It is not as easily accessible as being in the tabloid press and displayed on a newspaper stand. As the injunction remains in place, if you want to know the names you'll need to do your own search!

The above cases are useful illustrations because they involve both private and public interests. Although Pound suggested that the public interest would prevail when balanced against private interests it is clear from **Campbell**, **Murray** and **V** that this is not always the case. In **PJS**, the court made a neat distinction between the public interest and the interests of (members of) the public. In the first case the balance may tip towards the public interest but otherwise the law will favour the celebrity's private interests against the interests of inquisitive members of the public.

Look back at the data protection examples for more on privacy, e.g., the **Watson** and Amnesty cases highlight the balance between privacy (private interest) and security (public interest). I have not repeated them here as they are in every chapter so far.

The right to liberty and a fair hearing under Article 5 and Article 6 ECHR: the rule of law and terrorism

The **Anti-terrorism, Crime and Security Act 2001** allowed the Home Secretary to detain indefinitely foreign nationals suspected of terrorism, without charge or trial.

The then Prime Minister, Tony Blair, said he had to

> *"... weigh the wrong which is being done to a tradition in history of the primacy of law versus the wrong that would be done were any of these terrorist organisations to succeed in their ambitions."*

The Law Society said

> *"We recognise the government has a difficult balancing act. But it is essential that emergency terror legislation protects the country without compromising the government's duty to uphold fairness and justice."*

The **Act** was passed and in an appeal in 2004 by several suspects who had been held for three years without trial, the HL held it was against the rule of law and breached the **ECHR**.

In **A v the Home Department 2005** (known as the 'Belmarsh case' after the prison where suspects were held), Lord Hoffman said, in response to government arguments that the Act was necessary to protect the life of the nation,

> *"The real threat to the life of the nation ... comes not from terrorism but from laws such as these".*

He indicated that terrorism had succeeded if it meant the country rejected the rule of law in response to threats of terrorism. The **ECHR** allows for derogation from **A 5** if there is a public emergency threatening the life of the nation and the powers granted were necessary in the situation. The HL held that the first part was satisfied but on balance found the powers to hold suspects without charge indefinitely to be unnecessary. There were other options such as tagging or curfews. The HL also noted that the power only applied to foreign nationals and could not see how locking up foreigners could be justified when nationals who represented the same kind of threat would not be locked up. A declaration that the law was not compatible was made and the **Terrorism Act 2006** removed the indefinite detention. It still allowed for suspects to be held without charge for 28 days and this was increased to 42 days by the **Counter-Terrorism Act 2008**. The **Protection of Freedoms Act 2012** has reduced it to 14 days. The interests of society in wanting to be protected have to be balanced not only against the suspect's rights, but also against the other interests of society in living in a free and fair state, and of justice as a whole and the need to uphold the rule of law. We all want to be safe, but most people do not want to live in a society that can lock people up without any charges being brought against them. A criminal trial is the proper place to decide these issues.

The courts do not favour individual rights over the public interest in terrorism cases if the restriction of the freedom is less severe. In **Beghal v DPP 2015**, a woman was stopped by police on arrival at East Midlands airport and questioned for several hours. There were no grounds for suspicion other than that her husband was in custody in France on charges of terrorism. She argued that this conflicted with her rights under the **ECHR**. The case went to the SC which balanced her interests against those of the state to be protected against harm. On balance the SC held that the actions of detaining her were both proportionate and legitimate and that most international travellers expected some kind of interference with their rights in the interests of safety. Allowing such actions by the police achieved a fair balance between her private interests and the public interests of the community at large. In **Miranda v Home Department 2016**, the CA referred to **Beghal** and again held the actions of stopping a journalist at Heathrow and removing data from him to be lawful and proportionate under UK law. However, in this case the court issued a declaration of incompatibility with **A 10**.

Most of the freedoms (or rights) under the **ECHR** have what are called 'derogations'. This means that they may be sacrificed in the interests of, e.g., state security or public health. In this case, individual rights are subordinated to the public interest. Thus the right to liberty and the right to a fair hearing under **A 5** and **A 6** can be restricted by anti-terrorism laws in the interests of security, as in **Beghal**. Freedom of expression under **A 10** not only has to be balanced against an individual's right to a private life under **A 8** as discussed above, but also against the public interest There are therefore laws which restrict this freedom, e.g., the **Official Secrets Act**, blasphemy and censorship laws, defamation laws etc. In all criminal cases there is a restriction on freedoms as a suspect can be detained for certain amounts of time without charge, even though supposedly innocent until found guilty in a court of law. Fingerprints, photographs and DNA samples can also be taken and this material can also be retained indefinitely where someone has been convicted of a recordable offence. In **Gaughran 2015**, a man pleaded guilty to driving with excess alcohol and then challenged the policy of retaining samples on the basis that it conflicted with **A 8**. The SC decided that the public interest in retaining the data outweighed his private interest under **A 8**. Although a blanket policy of holding such data indefinitely could conflict with **A 8,** the SC decided that on balance the policy was justified in the circumstances.

The following are a few examples of some of the different issues that can come under **A 8**.

The aspect of private life involved	**Case examples**
The storage of embryos for fertilisation at a later date	**Jefferies 2016**
The right to die	**Nicklinson & Another 2013 / Conway v SS for Justice 2017**
The withdrawal of treatment	**Re M 2011 / M v A Hospital 2017 / PL 2017**
The force-feeding of an anorexic	**Re E 2012**
The smoking ban in prisons	**Black v the Secretary of State for Justice 2015**
Allowing children who are 'Gillick competent' to make decisions for themselves	**Gillick v West Norfolk and Wisbech AHA 1986 / Axon v Secretary of State for Health 2006**
Data protection	**Home Secretary v Tom Watson & Others 2016 / Andrew v MPC 2017**

Examination tip

Cases where the interests are the same but the balance has tipped different ways are useful. You can identify the interests and then explain how they compete and why the court made the different decisions. There are several examples in the previous section on privacy and the media. Another is the conflict between the right to liberty and a fair hearing and public safety.

Task 25

Identify the rights in **A v the Home Department** and **Beghal** and explain how the law balanced these rights. Why did the courts come to different decisions when balancing the interests?

Evaluation pointer

It is not always clear what an appropriate balance *is*. Look at the notes you made for the tasks. Did the laws you chose achieve an appropriate balance? Was justice achieved? For everyone, or just one of the people involved? These are difficult issues and it is unlikely the law will always get it right. It is often the case in life that if you try to please everybody you end up pleasing nobody and the law is no different.

Task 26

Would it be acceptable to torture a suspected bomber to get the location of a bomb which could kill hundreds of people? Apply the utilitarian theory of justice. Now go on to consider whether it is in the interests of society and whether this outweighs those of the individual? Is society itself degraded by such treatment?

Don't panic, there is no 'right answer' here. Just jot down your thoughts.

5.4 The legal process

Competing interests will be seen at various stages during the law-making process. The government has to balance these when formulating policy to put into a draft bill, as with the public consultations preceding the **Human Fertilisation and Embryology Act 2008**.

Also when making a bill, the **Human Rights Act 1998** affects the balance between the potentially competing interests of the state and the people. This **Act** ensures that rights under the **European Convention on Human Rights** are taken into account when the policy is drafted into a Bill. Also, the Green and White consultation papers allow for different interest groups to be consulted at this stage. The resulting law may well reflect their interests. During the process of the Bill becoming an Act, various bodies will be lobbying Members of Parliament to vote in their interests. Finally, judges have to interpret and apply an Act once it becomes law. The **Human Rights Act** has an influence on the balance here too because judges must take the **ECHR** into account when interpreting laws.

The **Police and Criminal Evidence Act 1984** (**PACE**) was an attempt to achieve a fairer balance than previously was the case by giving people various rights following arrest. The law recognises that those arrested are in a weaker position while in police custody so need some protection. When deciding on what rights to provide (like the right to a solicitor) the law balanced the suspect's interests with the interests of the police (in being able to investigate crime effectively). The rights given to suspects by **PACE** impose a corresponding duty on the police, e.g., to provide access to a solicitor and abide by the rules on custody. The right to a fair hearing under the **ECHR** is balanced against the corresponding duty to ensure there is an independent judiciary, trial by jury and a chance to examine witnesses (as well as the right to legal advice under **PACE**). The public interest is taken into account, too.

The right to a trial by jury has to be balanced against the cost of providing such trials. In the interests of justice the balance has usually tipped in favour of the individual's right to a fair trial. A bill to remove complex fraud trials from being heard by a jury was enacted but never became law. The **Protection of Freedoms Act 2012** repeals these provisions. However, it does not affect the **Criminal Justice Act 2003**, which allows for trial without jury where there are fears of jury tampering. Here the balance has tipped in favour of protecting members of the jury and the first trial without jury in a major criminal case took place in January 2010. The other area where a balance has been sought between cost and justice is legal aid. Previous laws increasing access to justice were an attempt to balance the rights of the public to protection from civil or criminal behaviour which caused harm with those of D to have a chance to get legal aid and advice to bring or defend a case. The **Legal Aid,**

Sentencing and Punishment of Offenders Act 2012 (LASPO), has severely reduced access to justice and legal aid, especially in civil cases. This has tipped the balance a long way from D's private interests towards the public interest in saving money. See Chapter 2 for more on this.

Here are a few more examples of competing social and private interests in the legal process.

Alternative Dispute Resolution

- An attempt to balance interests through negotiation, mediation and conciliation. The Woolf reforms also ensure judges act as mediators.

Trials

- The right of D to be tried by ordinary people balanced against the cost to society of a jury trial.

Bail

- There is a presumption that bail should be granted in most cases. This achieves greater justice for the accused, who is deemed innocent until found guilty. The presumption does not apply in murder and rape cases. D's rights are subordinated to those of society to be protected from such serious crimes.

Precedent

- The public interest in punishing criminal behaviour must be balanced against D's interests. Justice requires that D is only convicted if at fault. Thus, in **Gemmell and Richards 2003** the HL used the **1966 Practice Statement** to overrule its own earlier decision.

5.5 Sanctions and remedies

These will be relevant when considering *how* a balance is achieved. The public interest is often seen in sentencing (sanctions) policy. When deciding on appropriate remedies the judge will try to engineer what Pound called *"the maximum number of wants with the minimum amount of friction and waste"*.

Sentencing

A deterrent sentence may sacrifice the interests of the particular D to those of society. For example, a custodial sentence may be given where the offence does not really warrant one. It is used to stop re-offending and deter others from offending, thus protecting society. A crime against children or the elderly often leads to a public demand for a harsher sentence; here the community interest may outweigh D's. V's private interests are also weighed in the balance, and courts will take into account a Victim Impact Statement, showing the effect of the crime on V.

Remedies

When deciding on appropriate remedies, especially equitable ones such as an injunction, the judge must balance the competing rights of the individual parties in an attempt to find a just solution. The community interest may affect the balance. The law acts as mediator, and the judge will attempt to achieve a compromise which will most satisfy all interests. Look at **Miller v Jackson**. The court allowed her claim but refused to grant an injunction to stop the cricket. She received damages to compensate her for past and future inconvenience but an injunction was refused, which meant the cricket could continue.

Task 27

Choose any of the procedures. Write down the competing interests involved and how the law engineered a balance between these interests. Now consider which theories of justice would most support this balance. Keep this for revision of both areas.

Examination tip

Try to discuss interests outside the obvious claimant/defendant or defendant/victim roles. These are certainly valid examples but there are many wider issues. A common point made in examiners' reports is that students often fail to refer to the wider impact on society.

Summary

- **Pound saw law as an engineering tool**
- **The law balances interests to regulate how society behaves**
- **The law must balance public and private interests when making law (as illustrated by influences on Parliament, the consultation process, taking human rights into account etc.) and when regulating the legal process (as illustrated by rules on bail, access to justice, custody, jury trials and mediation)**
- **The law must also balance public and private interests when applying law (as illustrated by the examples from crime, tort, contract and human rights)**
- **The law balances interests in an attempt to achieve justice for the people concerned**

- **Achieving justice can be difficult as one person's interests may affect the interests of others. With rights come corresponding duties**

- **The balance may be affected by the different views of justice of those making or applying the law. The utilitarian view would be to maximise happiness but the natural law view would be to ensure the law had a moral content.**

Self-test questions

1. *What does Pound mean by saying that law is an engineering tool?*
2. *Give one example from civil* **or** *criminal* **and** *one from the legal process where you can explain the competing interests*
3. *What effect does the* **Human Rights Act** *have on court cases?*
4. *How would a utilitarian engineer the balance between competing interests?*
5. *What happened in* **Miller v Jackson** *and whose interests prevailed?*

For answers to the tasks and self-test questions, please go to my website at www.drsr.org and click the button 'Answers to Kindle tasks'

6.1 A general guide to revision

The first and foremost rule for revision is to start early. Too many students leave it until the last minute and then panic. If you take it gently and organise your time properly you will feel a lot calmer and more confident when exam time comes. Make a plan of what you want to cover each day and try to stick to it. Don't forget to include some breaks in your schedule. If you are tired it will be harder to retain the material you have been revising.

Here are a few tips for revision techniques:

- ***Go through your notes and try to summarise them***
- ***Learn cases for each topic especially where you can use them to illustrate several concepts***
- ***Make sure you understand how the judge has applied the law to the facts***
- ***Make sure you understand any problems the case raises or solves***

Example

In **Brown**, the judges decided that consent was not a defence to serious harm.

It raises a problem in the law, because the reasoning was obscure. Justice requires clarity in the law and it was not sufficiently clear why the consent defence failed. It could be argued that the defence fails if harm was intended (this would apply to **s 18** but not **s 20**), or alternatively that the defence fails if harm was serious (this would apply to both **s 18** and **s 20**). Intention relates to fault as it is the mental element of the offence. The acts were consensual so the element of fault was low but the conviction was for grievous bodily harm.

Another problem relates to the concept of law and morals. Some of the judges seemed to rely on their own moral values when reaching their decision. According to the positivist view of justice, law and morals should be separate. The decision that they were guilty does not appear to satisfy either utilitarianism or distributive justice, though natural law might support it.

A further problem is whether the law balanced the interests fairly and whether justice was achieved. The competing interests were the men's private interests to act as they chose which had to be balanced against the public interest in prohibiting immoral behaviour. The activity took place in private, so the burden on the men of a criminal conviction arguably outweighed any public benefit in finding such behaviour illegal. There was not a fair distribution of burdens and benefits and personal autonomy was subordinated to the community interest. Justice was not achieved on the distributive or libertarian theories though would be under natural law.

- ***Go through the summaries of the topic. These provide a base of the essential points which may need to be addressed***
- ***Go to the examination board's website for past exam papers, mark schemes and reports***
- ***Practice answering questions then look at the examiners' mark schemes and reports to see if you were on the right track***

There is an overlap between the various concepts of law, especially morals, justice and balancing competing interests. When revising each one, think about whether a case can be used for more than one theory, as in **Brown** above. Killing is a matter of both law and morals and murder and manslaughter are both illegal, as are assisting a suicide and active euthanasia. Justice according to natural law should be based on morals and so protect all life. Under this view of justice assisting a suicide and euthanasia should not be made lawful. There are plenty of case examples on this in Chapters 2, 3 and 5. **A 2** of the **ECHR** protects the right to life and has been relied on in some euthanasia cases where the legal rules are unclear. Balancing interests (personal autonomy against the sanctity of life) often comes into these cases. People have argued that **A 8 ECHR** should allow them to choose the time and manner of their own death, i.e., a 'right to die' rather than a right to life under **A 2**. An example is **Conway v SS for Justice 2017**.

Task 28

Choose a case of your own and make a note of how you would relate three or more of the different concepts to it. If you can't relate all of them don't worry, not all cases involve, e.g., a question of morals. Keep this for revision.

What follows is a brief summary of each concept for revision.

6.2 Revision of law and morals

The main differences between moral rules and legal rules are:

Moral rules

- develop through opinions over time and don't change overnight
- ought to be obeyed
- are enforced by peer pressure and self-guilt
- are voluntary and apply to those who agree to be bound by them

Legal rules

- can change instantly by Act of Parliament or precedent
- must be obeyed
- are enforced by the courts imposing sanctions
- are not voluntary and apply to everyone

There are different views as to how far the law and morals should overlap. These are covered with justice below.

Sometimes the law has to be involved in moral issues because of a dispute between individuals, as in **Quintavalle**.

Sometimes the law changes to reflect changing moral attitudes, as with the legalisation of prostitution following the Wolfenden Committee report.

Task 29

Find another example of the law changing to reflect moral values and explain how it changed.

The next paragraph is not revision. It is material I cut from Chapter 2 because I felt there was too much on crime and morals. You can leave it out if you like.

Euthanasia

It is legal in Belgium, so many people travel there to avoid the possibility of loved ones being prosecuted. An example is Bob Cole in 2015. He was dying and went to Belgium with four friends to a clinic where he would be given a lethal injection. He said he should have been allowed to die "*in my own country in my own bed*". One of his friends spoke of the UK law, saying "*the law is outrageous and immoral*".

Belgium became the first country to allow euthanasia for children in 2014. Although no age limits are set, the bill says that the child must have "*a capacity of discernment and be conscious at the moment of the request*". This is similar to the law in England on other kinds of treatment, which requires children to be 'Gillick' competent before being able to make decisions on medical care.

There was much heated debate prior to the passing of the Belgian law, with church leaders and other groups arguing that the law is immoral. It only applies where a child is terminally ill, and has made repeated requests to die. The child must also face "*unbearable physical suffering*" before euthanasia is considered as an option. Parents, doctors and psychiatrists would have to agree before a decision is made.

The relationship between law and morals can be divisive. In the United States euthanasia is legal in some states and not in others which means people who wish help to die may have to move away from friends and family to a state where prosecution can be avoided. In November 2014 a 29-year-old woman dying of brain cancer moved from North Carolina to Oregon so that she could "*die with dignity*". She was fortunate in that her friends and family were able to be with her, but not everyone can afford the trip. The Vatican said her actions were "*reprehensible*". In some of the high-profile UK cases the Oregon law would not help, because although it goes further in allowing assistance in the form of providing the drugs, the person wishing to die has to self-administer them. It is still illegal for a doctor to do so, and self-administering the drugs is not possible for those who are paralysed.

6.3 Revision of law and justice

Natural Law considers a just law as coming from a higher source (Aquinas/Aristotle)

- The source of law is above us so we should obey it
- Only law based on moral rules must be obeyed

Positivism considers law as coming from those authorised to make law e.g., Parliament or the courts (Kelsen/Hart)

- If a law is made correctly by those in authority, we must obey it, regardless of any moral content
- If we do not obey it, sanctions will follow (corrective justice)

Procedural justice looks at whether the legal process is just

Substantive justice looks at whether the law itself is just

Utilitarianism considers justice as based on the consequences of the law (Bentham)

- Justice is achieved by a law that produces the maximum benefit for the greatest number
- Individual rights are unimportant; the law is just as long as the majority benefit

Libertarian and egalitarian theories developed utilitarianism to consider quality of life not just quantity

- Mill thought people should be free to choose what they do unless it causes harm to others
- Law should only prohibit activities that harm others, rather than behaviour that is immoral or offensive

Distributive justice is seen in economic theories which are based on the distribution of wealth and property

Rawls saw justice as achieved where wealth and property is fairly distributed by the state – based on equality

Nozick saw justice as achieved where wealth and property is come by fairly – even if this did not produce equality, the state should not intervene

Marx would want the state to intervene to ensure a distribution that shared wealth and property according to need

Example

In **Rogers v Swindon NHS Primary Care Trust**, the problem was one of economics. Hospitals have limited resources and drugs can be expensive. If someone needs costly treatment, should it be made available? Rawls would want to see resources shared equally, which would deny the treatment to an individual. Marx would want any distribution of resources to depend on the needs of the individual patient, but would advocate that the money should come from those able to pay (*"from each according to his ability, to each according to his needs"*). In both views, the state should intervene to ensure a just distribution. However, in practice resources are limited so it will be difficult to achieve justice for all.

Task 30

Using examples briefly explain corrective justice.

6.4 Revision of law and fault

Remember to consider not only how important fault is in criminal and/or civil law but also how far it should be. Remember too that you may need to discuss strict liability, or liability without fault.

Here is a summary of the main points

- The main fault element in criminal law is *mens rea*
- Intention is the highest level of fault
- For most crimes the level of fault is subjective recklessness
- Manslaughter has a lower level of fault and can be committed by 'gross negligence'
- Defences can reduce or even remove the fault element
- Mitigating and aggravating factors indicate higher or lower levels of fault which can thus affect the sentence
- 'State of affairs' crimes do not require any fault at all, D can be liable just for being in the wrong place at the wrong time
- The main fault element in contract is breach of the agreement
- The main fault element in tort is negligence, not reaching the required standard of care
- Professionals have a higher duty, children a lower one (Bolam, Mullins)
- There is an element of fault seen in causation, as this requires foreseeability of harm
- In nuisance the fault element is that D has 'unreasonably interfered' with someone's enjoyment of land
- Motive is not usually relevant in finding liability, but can be in nuisance if malice is shown – Christie v Davy
- Strict liability is liability without fault and applies in both criminal and civil law

You will need to be able to select some cases and discuss the level of fault and whether the court made the right decision based on that fault. Here are a few examples from the criminal law.

Criminal case	Criticism
Savage	She did not intend harm so should have been guilty of battery not ABH
Khan & Khan	They should have been guilty of manslaughter as she would not have died if they had sought medical help. They showed more fault than Stone & Dobinson who were found guilty
Clinton	He should have been guilty of murder not manslaughter because he clearly intended to kill her, the highest level of fault
Blaue	He should have been guilty of murder not manslaughter because there was intent to seriously injure which is sufficient fault for murder
Majewski	He did not really know what he was doing and being reckless in getting drunk is not as blameworthy as being reckless as regards the offence
Meah v	He did not know there was caustic soda in the lemonade so should not have been guilty
Harrow LBC v	The shopkeeper did not know his employee had sold the ticket to someone underage so should not have been guilty
Winzar	He did not voluntarily commit any offence, so was not at fault. Therefore he should not have been criminally liable

Task 31

Choose five cases from tort and do the same as the above table from crime, adding a criticism of the decision.

6.5 Revision of balancing competing interests

Where interests are in conflict, the law will try to engineer a balance which will achieve social cohesion.

The purpose of the law is to satisfy as many interests as possible (the utilitarian view).

Society needs law to regulate the conflicts that arise between different interests. Law is a way of engineering how society behaves (Jhering/Pound).

Both public and private interests may need to be balanced.

Public and private interests should not be balanced against each other (Pound).

In practice neither Parliament nor the courts follow this idea.

Any attempt to balance interests on different levels would mean the dominant interest prevails and this is likely to be the public one (as in **Miller v Jackson 1977** and **Brown 1994**).

A utilitarian would want to see the balance made so as to achieve the greatest happiness for the greatest number.

There are many cases in the substantive law of crime, contract and tort. However, the area that probably produces the most examples is human rights law. When protecting such rights the law needs to perform a balancing act because one person's freedom may clash with another's.

Since the passing of the **Human Rights Act 1998**, incorporating the **European Convention on Human Rights** into English law, private interests have been given greater priority. However, a person's rights to, e.g., respect for a private and family life may restrict not only the freedom of another, but also the public interest. This is because people have a legitimate interest in knowing about celebrities' lives. Fame comes at a price and the price is some loss of privacy. However, the courts will take the circumstances into account and do not always decide that the right to privacy trumps freedom of expression. This can be seen in the different way the balance fell in cases such as **Campbell**, **AAA v Associated Newspapers**, **Murray**, **Ferdinand** and **Weller**.

Most of the Articles of the Convention have derogation clauses which allow the public interest to take precedence in cases of national security, public safety and health. Thus, even where private interests are protected by law the public interest may still outweigh those interests. Again, the courts will take the circumstances into account. You can use terrorism and data protection cases as examples of this.

Task 32

In deciding how successful / effective the law is in balancing interests one can look at cases and situations where public interests and private interests conflict. Pound's view was that public and private interests should not be balanced against each other. Any attempt to balance interests on different levels would mean the dominant interest prevailed, which is likely to be the public interest.

Bearing this in mind, briefly state how effective you think the law is in balancing the competing interests in the following examples. Then add a brief general paragraph on how successful the law has been in balancing interests which could be used as a conclusion in an essay.

- ***The mandatory life sentence for murder***
- ***The Consumer Rights Act 2015***
- ***Anti-terrorism laws***
- ***Watts v Herts CC***
- ***Conclusion***

Chapter 7: Examination practice

This book covers the nature of law for both the AQA and Eduqas examinations. Although the concepts are the same for both examination boards the focus and marks differ. There is more on the specifics for the question styles under "Example questions". I have explained the main requirements for each board first and then followed this by some general examination advice and then the example examination-style questions.

7.1 About the AQA examination

The main thing to know for the AQA examination is that from 2019 there is no longer a paper for the nature of law (concepts of law). There is not even a separate section in a paper, and maybe not even a separate question. There are two mixed questions on each paper and these will combine the substantive and non-substantive law. One of these questions (Q 9) is on general legal theory / the English legal system or one of the concepts but this non-substantive law needs to be discussed in connection to the substantive law. In the sample materials AQA produced in 2017 Q 9 on Paper 1 asked whether the exclusion of sexual infidelity in the loss of control defence achieves justice. The second question (Q 11) is based on a scenario but also requires a discussion of theory / the English legal system or one of the concepts in connection to the scenario. In the 2017 specimen papers the non-substantive law in Q 11 was the English legal system for Papers 1 and 2 and concepts of law for Paper 3.

All this means that the theory or nature of law will come onto each of the three papers on crime, tort and human rights or contract. There may therefore be three questions on three of the four concepts. It is important to study all four as you won't be able to guess what will come up.

There is further guidance and a full examination paper in each of my books, Criminal law for AQA AS and A level, Tort Law for AQA AS and A level (both published by Create Space in 2017) and Human rights law for A level (publication due in 2018). Here is a brief summary of what to expect.

There are three papers. Each is 2 hours long, worth 100 marks and is a third of the A Level. In each paper there are 75 marks for the substantive law and 25 for the non-substantive law. The non-substantive law includes the theory of law and the English legal system as well as the nature of law. The nature of law is allocated to the three papers as follows:

Law and society – fault: Papers 1 and 2

Law and society – balancing competing interests: Paper 3 (but note it is included in the substantive law for tort in relation to injunctions as a remedy)

Law and morality: Papers 2 and 3

Law and Justice: Papers 1 and 3

Although these concepts are assigned to a particular paper, you are not limited to using only that area of law to illustrate the concept.

For each paper there are 5 multiple-choice questions on the substantive law and the English legal system (total 5 marks). There are 2 short answer questions at 5 marks each one on the substantive law and one on the English legal system (total 10 marks). There is one 10-mark question on the substantive law (total 10 marks). There is one 15-mark extended writing question on BOTH substantive (5 marks) and non-substantive law (English legal system or nature / role of law) (10 marks), total 15 marks. Finally, there are two extended writing questions at 30 marks each (total 60 marks). One of these is only on substantive law, the other mixes substantive (23 marks) and non-substantive law (English legal system or nature / role of law) (7 marks).

In each of the papers, you have to answer **all** questions. It looks like this:

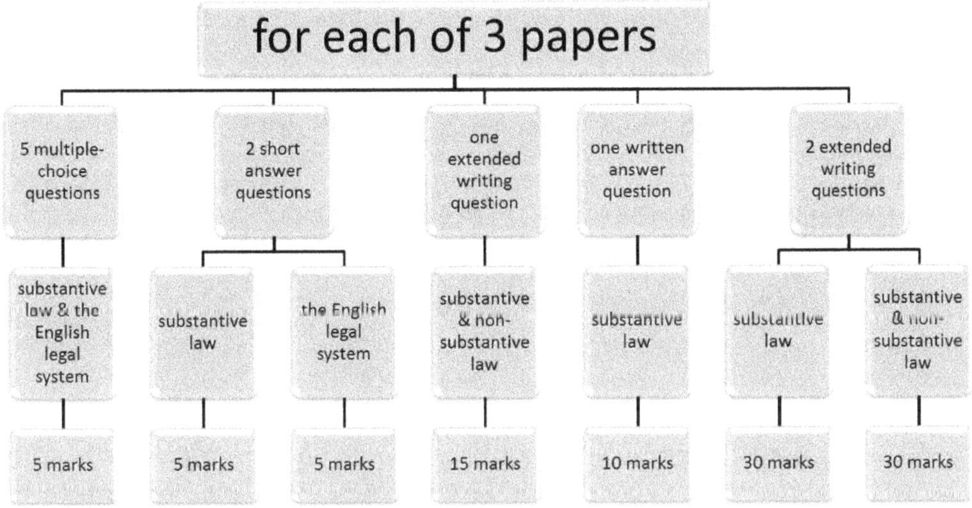

For specimen papers and mark schemes visit the AQA site at www.aqa.org.uk.

For teachers: Please visit my website at www.drsr.org for a Guide for teachers including the changes to the specifications and examinations.

7.2 About the Eduqas examination

There are three components to the Eduqas assessment in three separate papers.

The first component is law making, the English legal system and the nature of law (50 marks).

This gives a choice of questions. You must answer three out of four questions in Part A. Two are on an explanation of law making and legal rules and principles. You must answer both of these for 5 marks each. The third and fourth require you to apply legal rules and principles to a scenario and these questions include the nature of law. You must answer one of these two questions for 15 marks in total (shared between application and nature of law).

In Part B you must answer one out of two questions on the English legal system. Each has two parts, one on application for 10 marks and one on evaluation for 15 marks. The second part includes the nature of law.

Thus in Component 1 Part A and Part B are worth 25 marks each, making a total of 50 marks. This is 25% of the A level qualification.

The second component is the application of the substantive law (75 marks). There will be four sections with two questions on each of the four substantive law subjects. You must answer one question from each of three out of the four sections (25 marks each).

Thus in Component 2 each section is worth 25 marks making a total of 75 marks. This is 37.5% of the A level qualification.

The third component is on the evaluation of the four substantive law subjects (75 marks). Again you must answer three questions (25 marks each). These must be the same three subjects that you chose in Component 2.

Thus in Component 3 each section is worth 25 marks making a total of 75 marks. This is 37.5% of the A level qualification.

Eduqas examination papers are now called components.

The first component on the non-substantive law is 90 minutes long. When revising for the examination Eduqas students should focus on the legal process examples in each chapter of this book to illustrate a discussion of the nature of law for Component 1. However, the substantive law examples will help you use the various concepts when evaluating the law for Component 3.

The other two components are on the substantive law and are 2 hours 15 minutes each.

The substantive law is three out of four of the following subjects.

- Criminal law
- Law of tort
- Law of contract
- Human rights law

For specimen papers and mark schemes visit the Eduqas site at www.eduqas.co.uk

7.3 A general guide to examination papers (all boards)

Read **all** questions carefully even if you are given a choice.

Look again at the ones you wish to answer to make sure you can do so, make brief notes – this can be a useful checklist later when you are tired and your memory begins to fail.

Structure your answer. A solid start is worth a lot and gets the examiner on your side. A small plan is helpful.

It is necessary to do more than regurgitate your notes. Never put in irrelevant material just because you know it – there is **never** a question asking you to 'write all you know about...'. You need to select what is relevant, and choose appropriate cases and examples in support of what you say.

In essay questions, you will usually be asked to form an opinion or to weigh up arguments for and against a particular statement. Here a broader range of knowledge is needed showing arguments for, arguments against and an evaluation of these arguments. You should always round off your answer with a short concluding paragraph, preferably using some of the wording from the question to indicate to the examiner that you are addressing the specific issue raised.

Essays should have a logical structure. The beginning should introduce the subject matter, the central part should explain/analyse/criticise it as appropriate, and the conclusion should bring the various strands of argument together with reference to the question set.

Try to consider alternative arguments. A well-rounded essay will bring in other views even if you disagree with them; you cannot shoot them down without setting them up first.

Here is an idea of how to structure your essay.

7.4 Writing a discussion essay: staging the information logically

If you stage your essay as follows, it will make it easy to read, logically structured and easier to write. It may also mean you don't leave out important points. Here's how it works:

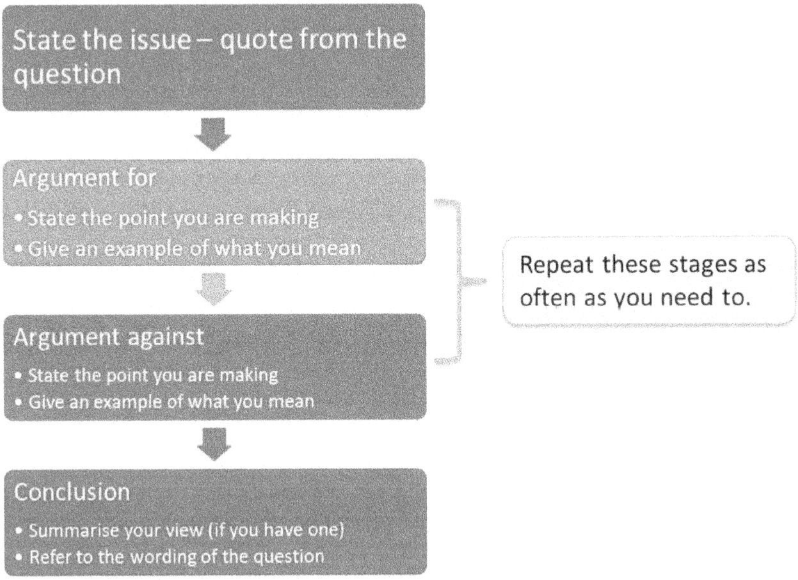

State the issue – quote from the question
Argument for
• State the point you are making
• Give an example of what you mean
Argument against
• State the point you are making
• Give an example of what you mean
Conclusion
• Summarise your view (if you have one)
• Refer to the wording of the question
Repeat these stages as often as you need to.

Writing each paragraph: making each one logical and easy to read (and write!). Here is an example for law and morals

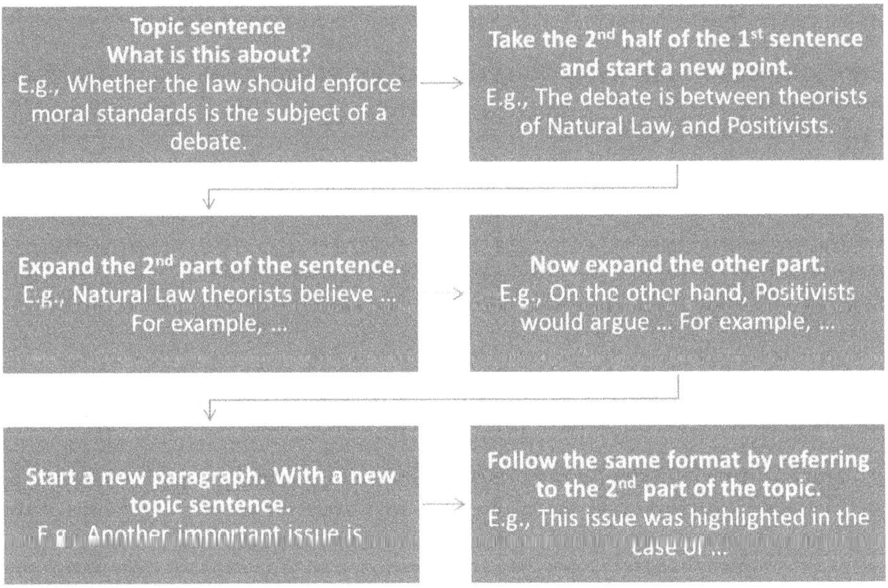

Topic sentence
What is this about?
E.g., Whether the law should enforce moral standards is the subject of a debate.
Take the 2nd half of the 1st sentence and start a new point.
E.g., The debate is between theorists of Natural Law, and Positivists.
Expand the 2nd part of the sentence.
E.g., Natural Law theorists believe ... For example, ...
Now expand the other part.
E.g., On the other hand, Positivists would argue ... For example, ...
Start a new paragraph. With a new topic sentence.
E.g., Another important issue is
Follow the same format by referring to the 2nd part of the topic.
E.g., This issue was highlighted in the case of ...

Finally, make sure you cover the whole question; there are only a certain number of marks available. The examiner has a mark scheme to work to, so however brilliant your answer to one part of the question is, missing out the other parts will severely reduce your total marks.

Examination tip

Examination questions may allow you to use **either** civil **or** criminal law, or sometimes both to illustrate your essay. Read the question carefully but if you are given the choice, whether you choose one area or discuss both, the marks will be the same. Whichever approach you take, make sure you answer the particular question and try to include some current issues where appropriate.

7.5 Examination practice questions

Examination tip

There is no 'right' answer to theoretical and evaluation questions, opinions vary and you can form your own – but **always** use some theories, cases and/or examples to back up what you say.

For AQA the nature of law comes into all papers but for a maximum of 10 marks. It is connected to the substantive law.

For Eduqas the nature of law comes into Component 1 and connects to law making in Part A, where Questions 3 and 4 have a total of 15 marks between the two. It connects to the legal system in Part B where Questions 5 and 6 have 10 marks for application and 15 for the nature of law.

AQA in their sample materials required discussion of a specified concept. Eduqas may or may not be specific as to which concept you need to discuss. In the sample papers in 2017 the two questions in Section A were on challenging delegated legislation and statutory interpretation and then added to each *"In your answer you should include consideration of law and society"*. Law and society includes fault and balancing competing interests as well as the rule of law. The mark scheme referred to all these. Specifically for the question on challenging delegated legislation that the government is not above the law and both Parliament and judicial review are means of enforcing this aspect of the rule of law. In addition, the law has to balance competing interests, both public (the state) and private (the individuals affected by the legislation). For the question on statutory interpretation, the application of statutory interpretation shows how the judiciary balances competing interests and identifies the different interests of parties to a dispute. In addition, the law also has to decide the extent to which fault should lead to criminal liability and will interpret the law as requiring fault unless it is clear that fault is not required.

In Section B the two evaluation parts to the questions were on the importance of magistrates and the importance of no-win, no-fee arrangements and added *"In your answer you should include consideration of law and justice"*. This is more specific. For the first you need to explain the meaning of justice and then relate this to the role of magistrates in upholding that justice. For the second you need to explain the meaning of 'justice' and then relate this to the extent to which no win, no fee arrangements achieve justice or create barriers to justice. In discussing justice for this second question you should also include reference to the rule of law because the question is on access to justice. The rule of law requires that everyone is equal before the law and should have access to justice.

The tasks in this chapter (and the answers on the website) should help you see the kind of content you should include for each of the concepts. You may need a different depth of response depending on the marks available and on whether it is in Part A or B on the Eduqas component or on the AQA paper. Look at the questions and guides and use them as a base so that you can adapt them as necessary. AQA connects to the substantive law and Eduqas to the non-substantive law and each chapter in this book has examples of both. The concept itself is the same for all examination boards and the examples given will help for evaluating other areas. In the sample materials AQA produced in 2017, one mixed question on Paper 1 asked whether the exclusion of sexual infidelity in the loss of control defence achieves justice. This would require a certain amount of evaluation of the substantive law, specifically the criminal defence of loss of control. Similarly with tort, an AQA question on fault could be useful when evaluating the rule in **Rylands and Fletcher**. These mixed AQA-style questions can therefore be used by Eduqas students for Component 1 (for the nature of law or legal theory part) and for Component 3 (for the evaluation of the substantive law part).

For either board you will not know what you need to connect to until the actual examination. I have therefore kept the examination practice tasks fairly general but provided an answer which uses a selection of topics (both substantive and non-substantive) to illustrate.

Before going on to some practice questions here is a general guide which can be adapted to suit. I have chosen euthanasia and assisted suicide to illustrate how justice can be discussed in questions about the substantive law and legal process. I chose this as there are so many cases which can be used to illustrate a range of topics. There are plenty of other case examples in each chapter so you can choose those you understand best. The idea is for you to see how you can use the theories of justice (which are the same whatever the question) to discuss how these relate to different areas of law and legal process (which will change).

AQA students may want to concentrate on the substantive law examples and Eduqas students on the legal process, there are plenty of each. However, students from either board can use substantive law cases to illustrate procedure and *vice versa*. Thus **Freaney 2011** relates to the substantive law of diminished responsibility and the use of juries in the legal system. The table below gives some more ideas of both substantive and non-substantive connections to justice.

The question topic	What you can discuss and example cases / procedures	Justice connections
Murder	*Mens rea* and intent to kill (**Gilderdale**, **Cox**, **Inglis** and **Gazeley**)	The law on assisted suicide attempts to achieve justice. The offence is not murder even though there seems to be intent to kill so corrective justice can put right any imbalance at the sentencing stage. However the law on assisted suicide is too uncertain.
Voluntary manslaughter	Diminished responsibility (**Inglis**, **Gilderdale** and **Freaney**) Loss of control (**Clinton**, **Dawes** and **Gurpinar**)	These partial defences are also attempts to achieve justice as the judge can fit the sentence to the circumstances. Defences and sentencing are forms of corrective justice
Defences of consent and duress	Do not apply to murder (**Howe** and **Hasan**)	The law upholds the natural law view of justice that the law should reflect morality
Sentencing	The problem of the mandatory sentence. The judge cannot take mitigating and aggravating factors into account (**Inglis**, **Gilderdale** and **Freaney**)	Having a separate law on assisted suicide as well as the partial defences is an attempt to achieve justice by giving the judge discretion in sentencing (a form of corrective justice)
Law-making (parliamentary process)	It can take a long time to get a bill through Parliament and made into law.	Justice requires the law to be certain and Parliament can better achieve this. It is fairer for a law to be made

	There have been lots of bills but no change in the law (any euthanasia cases and Assisted Dying bills)	following proper debate in a democratically elected institution
Law-making (types of bill)	Many times a private member's bill has been put forward. This is common with controversial issues (any euthanasia cases and Assisted Dying bills)	Parliament is the right place to make the law as it is more likely to reflect a wider range of moral values than is the case with a judge
Law-making (sources of law)	Murder still comes under the common law and arguably such a serious crime should be regulated by an Act of Parliament	As above
Law-making (delegated legislation)	Judicial review of delegated legislation allows those affected by the law to challenge it (**Pretty**, **Purdy**)	Judicial review is a form of corrective justice
The legal process (lay people)	Jury equity can lead to perverse verdicts but may do justice in the particular circumstances (**Freaney**)	Unpredictable verdicts mean the law is inconsistent which goes against the rule of law and justice. However, the jury can base a decision on what is morally right and thus achieve justice on the particular facts
The rule of law	(any assisted suicide cases)	The rule of law and justice both require that the law should apply equally and the law should be certain
General principles of criminal law	The SC has said the law is too uncertain (**Nicklinson**). The law is based on individual responsibility and personal autonomy (**Cox/Gazeley**)	One theory of justice is that the law must be certain (part of the rule of law). The libertarian view of justice favours personal autonomy
Statutory interpretation	The courts have to interpret the law and the **Coroners and Justice Act** has clarified it somewhat so this may be easier than before. However, the **Act** introduces new restrictions such as the exclusion of sexual infidelity as a trigger (**Clinton**, **Dawes** and **Gurpinar**)	The interpretation in **Clinton** etc. achieves greater justice for someone who has lost control in circumstances involving sexual infidelity. The judges used corrective justice to put right the imbalance
Precedent	The courts are reluctant to change the law and feel Parliament should do so (any assisted suicide or euthanasia cases)	If Parliament changed the law it could lay down strict rules and this would make the law less uncertain
Human rights	The right to life under **A 2 ECHR** and the right to a private and family life under **A 8** both indicate that the law should allow people to choose the method and time of their own death	Personal autonomy and the libertarian view of justice require that people should have greater freedom of choice

All these examples could also be used in a discussion of other concepts.

For morals, you can focus on the conflict between natural law and positivism and libertarianism. There is no agreement on whether the sanctity of life or personal autonomy should prevail. **S 2 Suicide Act** favours the natural law view whereas **A 8 ECHR** favours the libertarian view.

For fault, you can focus on *mens rea* and the law on intent. Arguably the higher level of fault justifies a life sentence, however, *mens rea* includes intent to cause serious harm and this offends against the correspondence principle.

For balancing competing interests you could focus on the conflict between the public interest in protecting everyone from harm and preserving life against the private interest in having freedom of choice. As with morals, you can also focus on whether the sanctity of life or personal autonomy should prevail. **S 2 Suicide Act** favours the natural law view whereas **A 8 ECHR** favours the libertarian view.

Task 33

Draw up your own table with a few cases you understand well and note the connection to different areas of law and the other concepts, as I have done for justice.

There is no answer for this task but it should give you something to refer to when revising each area.

Examination tip

Many exam boards suggest you should use current issues and developments in the law when answering questions on jurisprudence or concepts of law. The examination question may even require recent examples, as in the task on morals below. Keep an eye on current affairs and try to bring in some of your own ideas as to how far the law is, or should be, involved in issues of morality. As stated earlier, there is no right answer to these issues but if you offer your own view, avoid being too opinionated. Remember this is a law exam, so always use the theories, cases, Acts of Parliament and / or legal procedures to support what you say.

Don't say, 'I think smoking is immoral and people are stupid to do it and it hurts everyone so it is right that it should be banned'. Instead say, 'I think smoking is immoral because many people are offended by it. One role of law is to protect people from harm so the **Health Act** is right to ban it. Mill might agree because, although he supported personal autonomy, he also said this did not apply where harm could be caused to others. Smoking affects other people's quality of life, and possibly even causes physical harm through passive smoking. The **Health Act** is also a valid piece of legislation so, even though positivists like Hart do not believe the law has to have a moral content, they would say this law should be obeyed'.

There are many possible answers to all theoretical questions. The approach you take will depend on the theories and cases you best understand and can use to illustrate your answer. The following tasks should help provide you with some material for a question on the nature of law.

The answers are longer than I asked you for because they include a range of examples for you to choose from, from both the substantive and non-substantive law. For AQA you may need to use more examples from the substantive law to illustrate your answer and for Eduqas more from the legal process. The specific content for the substantive law or process will, of course, depend on the question set. The main thing for all questions is that you have addressed the points raised by the question and used relevant cases and laws to illustrate.

Morals

As I said, the main thing is that you address the points raised by the question. In the following question not only do you need to discuss whether the law should be involved in moral issues, but also it is vital that you use some modern examples to highlight why the debate concerning law and morality continues to be important in the 21st century.

Task 34

Write an essay (around 450- 500 words) on the statement below.

'Discuss how far the law should be involved in moral values. Assess why it may still be important to debate issues of law and morality in the 21st century.'

Justice

Justice is perhaps the hardest of the concepts to answer a question on because there are many different theories as to what justice means. I have therefore covered this in more detail. You won't have time to discuss everything but here is a guide to help you to structure an essay, which you can then adapt to the question set. When using cases to illustrate, you should select the examples that make sense to you. There may be a need to strike a balance between breadth and depth. As long as the answer is not superficial, and – most importantly – covers the specific question, a candidate who covers a greater number of theories and/or examples would be expected to do so in less detail.

If you wanted to explain the meaning of justice and highlight how difficult it is to achieve you could include some of the following points:

- ***Discuss the different meanings of justice e.g. in terms of fairness or equality***
- ***Discuss the theories of justice, e.g., natural law, positivism, utilitarianism, economic theories***
- ***Distinguish between different aspects of justice, e.g. distributive/corrective, substantive/procedural (Aristotle/Hart)***
- ***Discuss the need for distributive justice to achieve equality, e.g., access to justice, legal funding, consumer law (with a possible reference to economic theories of justice)***
- ***Discuss the need for justice in the substantive law, e.g., consumer protection and anti-discrimination laws to balance inequalities***
- ***Discuss the need for a just system of procedural law to ensure equality and fairness, e.g., access to justice and legal funding, jury trials, the rule of precedent to treat like cases alike***
- ***Discuss the need for corrective justice to ensure any injustice is put right, e.g., the CCRC, sentencing and remedies***
- ***Discuss the need for the law to help balance competing interests between parties to a dispute in order to achieve justice***
- ***Explain and evaluate the difficulties in achieving justice, these include***
    - ***The difficulty of providing justice in light of the disagreement as to what justice is with reference to the debates between natural law, positivism and utilitarianism***
    - ***The problem of distributive justice as regards what is a fair distribution, with reference to the economic theories***
    - ***The difficulty of achieving justice in substantive law and balancing competing interests satisfactorily in a complex and multi-cultural society, e.g., anti-terrorism laws, Re A, Quintavalle etc.***

- ○ ***The difficulty of reconciling utilitarian theories with individual rights (Bentham/Mill)***
- ***Provide a conclusion referring to the difficulties***

Task 35

Write an essay (around 400-500 words) on the meaning of justice, highlighting some of the difficulties the law has in achieving justice.

Fault

Here is a question on fault followed by a student essay in response. This is for 25-30 marks but I have used it because it includes a lot of examples you can choose from, which could be used for either board. It is from the old AQA specifications where the questions on the nature of law did not have to be connected to a specific topic, but has plenty of material that can be used. After this essay is a task on fault in civil law from my AQA book on tort. As mentioned earlier, this can be used by Eduqas students not only for a discussion of fault for Component 1 but also for an evaluation of tort for Component 3.

'It is a principle of fundamental importance in English law that there should be no liability without fault.'

Consider how far fault is an essential requirement of liability in English law, and discuss the suggestion that fault should be an essential requirement (25-30 marks)

There will never be a 'right' answer to such abstract concepts, but this is an example. It was done by one of my students for homework, not in exam conditions. You would not be able to cover this much, in particular you can reduce the number of examples and the facts of the cases. Pick out some of the cases you know, and the parts of her essay that make most sense to you, and develop your own answer. The answer covers the law very well, certainly in the top mark band. I have added a very brief comment at the end.

STUDENT ESSAY

Fault itself provides that an act does not make a person guilty of a crime unless his mind is also guilty. For someone to be deemed at fault, the *actus reus* (physical element) must be voluntarily or freely willed. This is because there have been instances where the *actus reus* was involuntary and the defendant was therefore not at fault nor liable. A case example of such an instant is the case of **Hill v Baxter (1958)** where the defendant was stung by a swarm of bees whilst driving, and lost control of his car. Such involuntary responses are known as reflex actions and cannot be helped.

However, an exception to this rule is state of affairs cases. In such cases, the defendant need not have formed the required *mens rea* (mental element), but will still be found liable. A case example is **R v Winzar (1983)** in which the defendant had been admitted to hospital, was found to be drunk and told to leave. Later he was found in a corridor of the hospital and the police were called to remove him. They took him outside onto the highway and then charged him with 'being found drunk in a public highway'. The defendant appealed but the Divisional Court upheld the conviction, stating that there was no need for the court to have any regard as to how he came to be there; the fact that he was there was enough.

When it comes to omissions, there is generally no liability to act even if the defendant is morally at fault. However, an exception to this has been created where the law has imposed a duty to act. For example, in the case of **R v Miller (1983)** where the defendant (a squatter) fell asleep on a mattress smoking a cigarette. The defendant was awoken by the flames, but instead of putting the fire out, he got up and went into another room and went back to sleep. As a result, the house was substantially damaged by fire, and the defendant was convicted of criminal damage. The House of Lords held that once the defendant awoke and realised what had happened, he came under a responsibility to limit the harmful effects of the fire. The defendant's failure to discharge this responsibility provided the basis for the imposition of liability.

Causation must be established for result crimes, as they determine fault and therefore liability. There are two types of causation; in fact and in law. Causation in fact is established if 'but for' the defendants actions the resultant consequences would not have occurred. For example, in the case of **R v White (1910)** the defendant intended to poison his mother by putting cyanide in her drink. She, however, actually died of a heart attack. Therefore, the defendant was acquitted of murder and convicted of an attempt to murder. Although the consequence that the defendant intended occurred, he did not cause it to occur. Causation in law must prove that the defendant was the 'operating and substantial' cause of the resultant consequences. In **R v Smith (1959)** the defendant (a soldier) stabbed the victim (a fellow soldier), resulting in the victim's death. On being charged with murder, the defendant argued that the chain of causation between the stabbing and the death had been broken by the way in which the victim had been treated. The victim had been dropped twice whilst being carried to the medical station; the medical officer, who was dealing with a series of emergencies, did not realise the serious extent of the wounds; and the treatment he gave him was 'thoroughly bad and might well have affected his chances of recovery'.

However, the court held that the defendant's stabbing was the 'operating and substantial cause' of the victim's death because the victim clearly died from loss of blood caused by the stab wounds inflicted by the defendant.

Criminal liability can sometimes depend on a chance result rather than on the defendant's level of fault. For example, in the case of **R v Blaue (1975)** the defendant stabbed the victim (a Jehovah's Witness) 13 times. The victim refused a blood transfusion on religious grounds and died from her wounds. The defendant was convicted of manslaughter and appealed because the victim had refused treatment and therefore broken the chain of causation. It was held that the defendant had to take his victim as he found her, meaning not just her physical condition, but also her religious beliefs. The question for decision was what caused the death. The answer was the stab wound. The same can be said about the case of **R v White (1910)**, whereby the defendant was only excused because his mother died of a heart attack before she had chance to drink his poison.

Mens rea must be established for most offences and shows blameworthiness. There are three types of *mens rea*, decreasing in the level of fault required.

Firstly, intention, which can either be direct (where the defendant desires the consequences of their actions, so is at fault and therefore liable) or oblique (where the defendant foresees the consequences of their actions as virtually certain and continues anyway).

Secondly, recklessness, which can be subjective (defendant must have realised that there was a risk, as in the case of **R v Cunningham (1957)**) or objective (defendant is compared to a reasonable person, as in the case of **MPC v Caldwell (1982)**). Objective recklessness requires less fault than subjective recklessness, which was shown in the case of **Elliott v C (a minor) (1983)**. In this case the defendant was only 14 and of low intelligence. She stayed out all night without sleep and entered a garden shed, which she set fire to. The Divisional Court reluctantly upheld her conviction for aggravated criminal damage, because the court was bound by the precedent set in **MPC v Caldwell (1982)**.

Lastly, negligence, which is falling below the standard of the reasonable person. The threshold for negligence ranges all the way to involuntary manslaughter. This was seen in the case of **R v Adomako (1994)**, where the defendant (an anaesthetist) had been left in charge but failed to notice that a tube leading from the patient to the ventilator had become disconnected. Unfortunately, he took the wrong action, which ultimately led to the patient's death. The defendant was convicted but appealed on the grounds that the *mens rea* should have been recklessness. However, the Court of Appeal was satisfied that a duty of care had been owed and that duty was breached.

However, some crimes do not require a form *mens rea* for every part of the *actus reus*, for example strict liability offences. In the case of **R v Prince (1875)** the defendant was found guilty of taking an unmarried girl under the age of 16 out of the possession and against the will of her parents, even though she looked older than her 13 years and told Prince that she was 18. The court stressed that the relevant section did not contain the words 'knowingly' or 'maliciously', so liability arose when Prince merely committed the act.

There can also be instances where fault does exist but liability can be extinguished by a complete defence, for example self-defence where a killing will be lawful if reasonable force was used to defend oneself. A case example is **R v Beckford (1988)** in which a policeman shot a man who had been terrorising his family. Similarly, the defence of insanity under the M'Naghten Rules states that if the defendant suffers from a defect of reason, from disease of the mind, as not to know the nature and quality of the act he was doing, or if did know it, that s/he did not know what s/he was doing was wrong. Proving either of these defences results in an acquittal.

Alternatively, liability can be reduced because of extenuating circumstances, which reflect a lower level of fault; for example, the Homicide Act 1957 and the Coroners and Justice Act 2009 create two partial defences to murder: diminished responsibility and loss of control. Proving either of these defences results in a reduced charge of voluntary manslaughter, which generally carries a lower prison sentence.

Finally, fault is relevant to the sentencing process whether the defendant pleads guilty or is found guilty. Firstly, the courts will consider aggravating factors, such as committing burglary with a firearm or imitation firearm, which might increase the defendant's sentence. It will also consider mitigating factors, which might decrease the sentence. Secondly, there can be a discount for an early guilty plea if the defendant admits s/he at fault. Thirdly, tariff sentencing reflects the defendant's blameworthiness. Fourthly, minimal sentences (in some circumstances) were introduced by the Crime (Sentences) Act 1997, although many judges are opposed to the Act because it fetters their discretion.

Unlike the statement suggests, It does seem that there sometimes is liability without fault, for example in state of affairs cases, where the defendant might not have voluntarily committed an act but will still be liable for it. Conversely, in omissions, there is generally no liability to act even if the defendant is morally at fault. Therefore, fault and liability do not always go hand in hand when it comes to English law. Arguably, fault should be an essential requirement in establishing liability, as it seems unfair to blame someone for something that they didn't mean to do (**R v Winzar (1983)**). Having said that, it also seems unjust to allow someone to get away with murdering someone, for example, just because they suffered from a defect of reason (**M'Naghten (1843)**).

Comments

I would put the explanation of fault and *mens rea* before *actus reus* and any exceptions to fault, as the question specifically asked for an explanation of fault. If you have studied civil law you may want to reduce the crime examples and add some civil ones (see next question). The conclusion is excellent. It nicely sums up what she has said and directs the examiner to the original quote in the question. This is always a good idea as it reminds the examiner that you are answering the question set, not the one for which you had a prepared answer.

N.B.: *The writer made an error in relation to insanity. This does not result in an acquittal but one of the 4 orders. This means a judge can take into account the level of fault when deciding which order is appropriate.*

The essay could benefit from some more recent examples and you will find plenty of these in Chapter 4. Other than that it is a top-grade answer showing a clear understanding of the topic.

The above answer focused on criminal law. The answer to the following question contains plenty of civil examples as it is from the tort examination paper in my book Tort Law for AQA AS and A level. It is based on a 15-mark question in the AQA sample materials. You should aim at around 600 words.

Task 36

Rylands v Fletcher is sometimes called a strict liability tort. Examine the significance of fault in establishing liability in civil law and discuss how far liability in **Rylands v Fletcher** is based on fault. 15 marks

Balancing competing interests

The main thing to remember when writing about competing interests and how the law may be used to balance them is to ensure you include the public interest. Criminal law protects society as a whole as well as individuals victims of crime. Civil law also takes account of the public interest, predominantly when public policy is taken into account as in the **Caparo** test and the social benefit factor in regard to breach of duty.

Task 37

Write an essay (around 400-500 words) on how the law balances competing interests and assess how effective it is in doing so

List of abbreviations

All these abbreviations are commonly used. You may use them in an examination answer, but should write them in full the first time e.g., write 'actual bodily harm (ABH)' and then after that you can just write 'ABH', similarly with the claimant (C) defendant (D) and the victim (V).

Case names should be in full the first time but can be shortened in later use if they are lengthy.

General

Draft Code – A Criminal Code for England and Wales (Law Commission No. 177), 1989

CCRC Criminal Cases Review Commission

ECHR European Convention on Human Rights

ABH actual bodily harm

GBH grievous bodily harm

D defendant

C claimant

V Victim

EU European Union

CA Court of Appeal

ECtHR European Court of Human Rights

HL House of Lords

SC Supreme Court

Acts and Treaties

S – Section (thus s 1 of the Occupiers Liability Act 1984 refers to section 1 of that Act)

s1 (3) means section 1 subsection 3 of an Act

ECHR – the European Convention on Human Rights

A – Article (thus A 2 of the ECHR refers to Article 2 of European Convention on Human Rights

In cases (these don't need to be written in full)

CC (at beginning) chief constable

CC (at end) county council

BC borough council

DC district council

LBC London borough council

AHA Area Health Authority

Judges and other legal personnel (these don't need to be written in full)

J Justice

LJ Lord Justice

LCJ Lord Chief Justice

LC Lord Chancellor

AG Attorney General

CPS Crown Prosecution Service

DPP Director of Public Prosecutions

AG Attorney General

Case index